Effective Business Communication

A Practical Guide

Effective Business Communication
A Practical Guide

Joseph Allen
Bennet P. Lientz

Goodyear Publishing Company, Inc.
Santa Monica, California

For our children
Andrew, Annie, Bennet, Charles,
Herman, and Johnny

Library of Congress Cataloging in Publication Data

Allen, Joseph, 1944–
  Effective business communication.

  Includes index.
  1. Communication in management. I. Lientz,
Bennet P., joint author. II. Title.
HF5549.5.C6A44   658.4'5   78-32083
ISBN 0–87620–236–9

Y–2369–0

Current printing (last digit):
10 9 8 7 6 5 4 3 2 1

Cover and Text Design: Richard Carter

Printed in the United States of America

Contents

8

Committees: Gang Writing

9

Oral Communication: Interviews And Presentations

PART IV
Doing Your Part

10
Reading For Meaning

11
Evaluating Yourself As a Communicator

12
Managing For Good Communications

Special Section: Using Communication Skills To Get That Job

Preface

This book grew out of a series of executive-level communication seminars conducted in industry and in graduate-level management classes. It is practical in its outlook and its applications, and we have attempted to avoid the "traditional" answers to problems wherever they were determined to be insufficient by the executives who participated in the seminars.

The operating premise of our approach is that the essence of communication is *meaning*. If meaning is not conveyed by any message, that message is a failure. Any message which adequately conveys the intended meaning—no matter what the format—is a success.

The flood of paperwork which threatens to engulf today's business world is largely the product of a devaluation of meaning. Only a person who had no interest in conveying meaning would write a confusing and thus useless memo or letter. Only a corporation which had no real interest in communication would foster—or allow—such writing.

Productivity seems to be the key to a healthy and expanding economy. In white-collar occupations, there is no possibility of productivity without useful and widely accepted norms of communication.

It is the experience of the authors that management is ready for a widespread upgrading of writing and speaking skills. The great multinational corporations are simply too large and too diverse to exist healthily without such skills. Government cannot long survive in anything like an effective mode without a reduction in meaningless paper. Small businesses and growing businesses cannot afford the luxury of white-collar illiterates.

Some of our suggestions are hard-nosed, but none of them are fanciful. We've attempted to write our approach in everyday language, not without humor. We've attempted to deal with problems not often mentioned in style books, grammar handbooks, writing manuals, and so on. But everything we've suggested is here because we consider it essential to the productive transfer of meaning between business associates and colleagues.

Nothing in this book restricts its use to either the private or the public sector. Our case studies and examples are drawn from fields as diverse as marketing, politics, job-hunting, office supply ordering, casual conversation, technical reporting, sales, government relations, and personnel.

We believe that today's businessperson will find EFFECTIVE BUSINESS COMMUNICATION entertaining and highly informative reading. Take it with you on the bus or train. Have lunch with it. There are no memory feats required. We won't lecture you on grammar or punctuation. What we will do is teach you to focus on your meaning, to convey your meaning, and to check to see that your meaning reached its mark.

This is a nuts-and-bolts approach. If you're looking to develop a high literary style, this book is not for you. If what you want to do is to learn to communicate more effectively, we can help.

The Special Section "Using Communication Skills to Get That Job," deals with resumes, letters of application, interviews, and self-analysis—in a way you will find accessible and relatively simple (nothing connected with getting a job is really simple).

We wish to acknowledge the invaluable aid provided us by several friends and colleagues. A deep and abiding debt of gratitude is owed by us to Ms. Nora Gordon, who read every word and kept the project moving. Heartfelt thanks are due to Prof. David Rodes, UCLA Department of English, for his comments and suggestions. We wish also to acknowledge the assistance provided by Prof. Jack McDonough, UCLA Graduate School of Management. A special debt of thanks obliges us to acknowledge the important contribution made by Margot Tommervik, a copy editor of unparalleled compassion and patience.

Joseph Allen
Bennet P. Lientz

MO:

_____

Part 1
Communication: The Particles of Meaning

1
The Transfer of Meaning

hat happens when you talk? Your brain coordinates a complex series of responses to the need to communicate, and intelligible sounds come out of your mouth. That's obvious. And that's easy. Much the same thing happens when you write, but the end product is marks on paper, rather than sounds carried through the air.

Talking and writing are not problems; they are simple motor skills. This book is not about talking and writing; it is about *communication*, which is, as they say, a whole new ball game.

Communication

Communication is the essence of business, the essence of social living. Without communication, capital wouldn't move. Products wouldn't be developed—or sold. Consumer demands wouldn't be expressed. Business would come to a standstill. Many major business ventures fail because of breakdowns in communication—like Ford's presumption that the public wanted the Edsel.

But everybody knows that. Communication problems (gaps, breakdowns, whatever we call them right now) are a recognized area of concern in the business community. Written communications especially are misstated, misread, misunderstood, and misinterpreted—not universally, but often enough to keep a steady stream of clarifying paperwork moving.

Communication problems are no problem to find; they're a problem to eliminate. Why do they happen—so consistently and so perniciously? There are many explanations; certainly there's an individual explanation for every misfire. But widespread communication problems aren't inevitable; they aren't unavoidable. It isn't an inherent quality of business that dead-sounding corporatese must become the official language of internal communications. It isn't an inevitable consequence of running a sales force that customers must be misinformed about the product. It isn't natural law that employees must write passive, reactive memoranda in prose that is unreadable and meaningless.

The emphasis in schooling over the past twenty years has been on various much-needed specializations. But, too often, the exceedingly difficult demands of these specializations have pushed aside the basics of education—reading and writing. And since the essence of business is that it involves more than one person, those reading and writing skills are sorely missed. The good communicator has become the exception, rather than the rule. So now it's become incumbent on the modern corporation to see to it that its employees can write, and a mighty task it is. But if the corporation can rise to the occasion, what marvels can be accomplished!

The caliber of American business personnel is constantly rising; even the poor grade of daily communication cannot obscure that obvious fact. Our scientists are faster, more perceptive, and more productive than ever. Our salesmen are go-getters, with better products to sell than have ever before been available. Our executives are a resourceful lot, able to deal with governmental and public environments that would have driven Jay Gould or John D. Rockefeller, Sr. to the brink of despair.

But in this burst of productive energy, some of the traditional humanistic studies have gotten short shrift. Foreign languages are seldom studied—so grammar is seldom understood. English is an elective not often elected, because it doesn't seem relevant. It is relevant. There is no relevancy in a literate society if its citizens cannot read and write. And deficiencies in reading and writing are what cause the communication breakdowns that puzzle us, plague us, eat away at our confidence—and at our profits.

And there's another problem. Communication breakdowns are symptoms of an underlying condition—a chronic disease of the mind that becomes more and more acute with each passing year.

A Disease of the Mind

It's not a brain disorder or a psychiatric malfunction; it's much more difficult to treat than either of these. It's that most horrifying of mass mental problems: a misconception. A truism that isn't true. A definition that doesn't define.

We've been taught all our lives that we speak and we write *to express ourselves.* We speak to express what we think, what we want. We type, write, telex to bring our needs, our likes, and our dislikes out in the open. Wrong. That's not what it's about at all. In some useful sense, that's what poetry is about, but it's not what communication is about.

Communication is a process by which we move an idea from one mind to another, intact. It isn't simply the meandering expression of one person's ideas or emotions; without that second mind—the mind of the receiver—communication doesn't exist. Without some transfer of information, what may be intended as communication simply becomes a self-satisfying string of sounds or written words. To say that communication is expression is like saying that a business transaction is payment: it is to ignore more than 50 percent of what goes on. A business transaction is not just payment. It may include payment, but it includes much more as well—negotiation, product, agreements, terms, time, delivery—the list could go on and on.

Communication includes expression; it also includes perception, retrieval of information, and impression. The sender of a message is responsible for it from the time he sends it until the time it is stored in someone else's brain. The message receiver's concern overlaps the sender's responsibility, but the receiver has no control over the message.

If this is beginning to sound complex—it actually isn't. The basic concept is this: somebody sends and somebody else receives. That sending and receiving—if it's done properly— manages to move an idea from the mind of the sender to the mind of the receiver. So simple that it's almost not worth belaboring, right? If the world operated in the way it ought to, instead of in the way it does, the basic communication relationship (sender to receiver) *would* be simple and would never be ignored. But in today's business world, unfortunately, that relationship is either forgotten or universally poorly handled.

The Communication Path

The illustration in figure 1.1 is a representation of a path followed by messages. An idea is put together in the mind of the sender (A); it is put into a medium; it is perceived by the listener (B), who tucks it away for future reference. But the pathway, as simple as it seems, is littered with dangers—broken glass, land mines. Tread carefully as you walk along it.

Communication is successful when a message is moved from A to B exactly intact. Communication fails when the message stored at B is in any way different from the message A sent. This

Figure 1.1. The communications path.

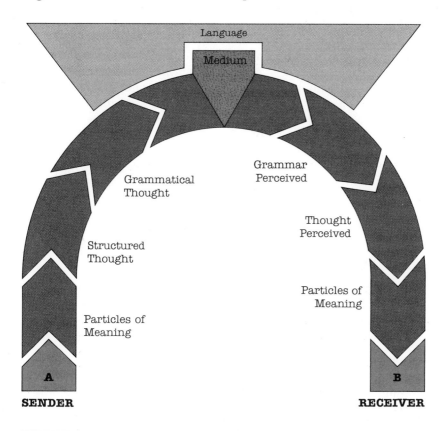

Language

Medium

Grammatical
Thought

Grammar
Perceived

Thought
Perceived

Structured
Thought

Particles of
Meaning

Particles of
Meaning

A

B

SENDER

RECEIVER

basic rule defining communication failure implies a multitude of evils. If the receiver understands less than you send, the message fails. If the receiver understands something different from what you send, the message fails. And if the receiver understands more than what you send, the message fails. Here are some examples:

Receiver Understands Less

Speaker says:
1. I need a truckload of methanol by next Tuesday.
2. John, Barbara, Pete, and Agnes all agree with me.
3. If I don't get my insulin, I will go into a coma.

Receiver understands:
1. Customer is ordering a truckload of methanol.
2. John, Pete, and Agnes all agree with you.
3. You need insulin.

Receiver Understands Something Different

Speaker says:
1. I need a truckload of methanol by next Tuesday.

Receiver understands:
1. Customer needs a truckload of ethanol by next Tuesday.

2. John, Barbara, Pete, and Agnes all agree with me.

2. John, Barbara, Pete, and Agnes are in agreement.

3. If I don't get my insulin, I will go into a coma.

3. You are going into a coma from lack of insulin.

Receiver Understands More

Speaker says:
1. I need a truckload of methanol by next Tuesday.

Receiver understands:
1. Customer will pay extra to have a truckload of methanol by next Tuesday.

2. John, Barbara, Pete, and Agnes all agree with me.

2. Everybody agrees with you.

3. If I don't get my insulin, I will go into a coma.

3. If you don't have insulin now, you will die.

All these messages are failures. In each case, the information stored by the receiver is different from the information intended by the sender. Whose fault is the breakdown? Maybe you ought to be sitting down to take this: it is always the sender's fault.

The Sender's Responsibility

It may seem a bit harsh to blame the sender whenever a message fails—but it is the only practical way to approach the problem. Compare this idea with some of the simple facts of business life. If a client rejects a sale because he was misinformed about the product, who carries the blame? The salesman, of course. If a bank fails to convey its annual percentage rate adequately and plainly to a borrower, who is held accountable? The bank, of course.

Despite the sender's responsibility being an everyday fact of life in the business world, it doesn't seem to have found its way into the consciousness of communicators. In reality, the very reverse is the popular belief: businessmen complain of people who "misunderstand" what they intended. From the sender's point of view, there can be no possibility of "misunderstanding"; there can only be messages that are missent.[1]

---

1. There are times, as we all know, when people "misunderstand" messages on purpose. But, then, they don't really misunderstand them; they just act as though they did, trying to avoid reality. And that's an entirely different problem.

Consider this: it is the sender who's trying to transmit information, whether at his own initiative or at the request of the listener. The form and substance of the message are entirely at the discretion of the sender; the receiver is only a receptacle into which information is deposited.

No one will pretend that the receiver of a message can remain entirely passive during communication. Unless some effort is expended in receiving, communication very seldom succeeds. But from the point of view of the sender, "You can't count on nothin'." An informed receiver provides a good assist to the sender; that goes almost without saying. But the sender is responsible for making absolutely certain that the message is received as transmitted. And, to the extent that the transmittal of information is important to the sender, that line of responsibility is frequently followed in spoken communication. Many speakers check for perception: "Do you understand what I said?" "Do you have any questions?" "Did I make myself clear?"

One of the troubles with written communication is that it is difficult to check for reception. In most cases, you don't ask your reader where he understands—or, if you do, you'll seldom hear his response until after the misunderstanding is complete. So there must be other ways of ensuring that messages are properly received. There are.

First, consider the following spoken conversation:

Ann. Bill, do you know where Kerry is?
Bill. Yes.
Ann. Well?
Bill. What do you mean?
Ann. Where is he?
Bill. Oh, he's at the lab, processing some film.
Ann. Why didn't you say so?
Bill. You didn't ask.

The pattern of Ann and Bill's conversation is familiar to everyone. Ann had to ask three questions to get an answer to her query about Kerry's location. Why? Certainly, it was reasonable for Ann to expect Bill to tell her Kerry's location from the original question. Many people would have responded, "Yes, he's at the lab, processing some film." But Bill didn't; he simply answered Ann's question—the way it was phrased. Ann made a fundamental error, despite the reasonableness of her question. She asked a question that did not express her real message. Ann's real message to Bill was "Where is Kerry?" If she had asked her question as "Where is Kerry?" she would have found out without the ensuing verbal Ping-Pong. The failure in the first question is Ann's. Ann then compounded the first failure by refusing to clarify her original message. Bill was puzzled. When, finally, Ann asked her real question—she got the answer she wanted.

Why spend time on a spoken problem that was resolved almost before it started? It presents us with a handy illustration of several principles that become overridingly important in written communication:

1. The sender must take responsibility for correct transfer of information.
2. The sender must not expect the receiver to decode a message that is formulated eccentrically or cryptically.
3. The sender must clarify fully at the first sign of bewilderment on the part of the receiver—which, when the sender is writing his message, is easier said than done.

Still, it seems like a tempest in a teapot, doesn't it? Perhaps. But consider what would have happened if the conversation had been held by memo, instead of face-to-face. It would have taken six written messages to do the work that two might have done. When you take a message (or series of messages) that's more complex than the Ann-Bill example—but follows the same pattern—you invest considerably more time and energy (and frustration) than necessary in your attempt to gather information. The series of interoffice memos in figure 1.2 illustrates just such a mix-up. Note the elapsed time between Linda's first memo and the final resolution of the problem.

Figure 1.2.   A series of interoffice memoranda.

Memorandum 1
To: William Shenks, Purchasing   February 23
From: Linda Monroe, Supply Clerk
Subject: Omega Office Supplies

We recently ordered some typewriter ribbons from Omega Office Supplies and were told that the supplies would be arriving soon, as they were on back order. This had happened each of the last three times we have ordered from Omega.

Memorandum 2
To: Linda Monroe, Supply Clerk   February 26
From: William Shenks, Purchasing
Subject: Your Memo of February 23

Thank you for pointing out the problems with Omega Office Supplies.

Memorandum 3
To: William Shenks, Purchasing   March 5
From: Linda Monroe, Supply Clerk
Subject: Omega Office Supplies

It has been some time since we last heard from you on our problems with Omega Office Supplies. Could you give us a statement on what action you have taken? The problems with Omega are still going on and we are really losing time and money waiting for supplies.

Memorandum 4
To: Linda Monroe, Supply Clerk   March 7
From: William Shenks, Purchasing
Subject: Omega Office Supplies

I have just received your latest memo dated March 5. Our previous correspondence has been reviewed. We did not realize that the back ordering was such a problem for your department. What action do you wish Purchasing to take with respect to Omega Office Supplies?

Memorandum 5
To: William Shenks, Purchasing   March 11
From: Linda Monroe, Supply Clerk
Subject: Omega Office Supplies

As I indicated in my first memo of February 23, we have been having problems getting supplies from Omega Office Supplies. This has been a recurring problem over the last month and a half. We would like you to take the appropriate action so that we can be assured of getting our supplies quickly after they are ordered.

Memorandum 6

To: Linda Monroe, Supply Clerk   March 16
From: William Shenks, Purchasing
Subject: Office Supplies

As you requested, we have contacted Omega Office Supplies and have indicated our concern with their service. They have promised to improve. We have also lined up an alternative supplier—Regal Business Supplies, 517 Holt, (411) 767-5479.

How Does the Communication Path Help?

The communication path helps you understand what happens to a message from the time you decide to send it until the time it's stored in the mind of the receiver. When you have a full understanding of this process, you'll be much better prepared to use it accurately—to send ideas in a form that will allow them to be understood and stored the way you want them understood and stored.

The first step in understanding the communication path is to recognize it as a natural pathway—not something we've created to prove a point. There's no other way for messages to be transferred from one mind to another. Ideas must be stored to be retrieved. They must be retrieved to be sent. They must be sent in an intelligible (that is, grammatical) form in an easily understood medium if they are to be stored for future retrieval and action. If any of these steps are faulty, the message will fail; the receiver won't understand.

Every communicating human being understands the communication path. The whole principle of language is imbedded in an understanding of it. You use it every time you open your mouth to say something. It's nothing new, although you may never have seen it depicted in precisely the way we've drawn it.

The Milestones Along the Way

Look back at figure 1.1, the graphic representation of the communication path. Let's have a look at each of the milestones marked on the illustration—and agree on some terms. The first term we encounter is *particles of meaning*; it is also the last term in the flow of information. Remember that a message that isn't stored exactly the way it was sent is a failed message. To the extent that the particles of meaning in A and in B are identical, the message has succeeded. What are particles of meaning? They are the smallest units of thought stored in your brain.

For our purpose right now, let's think of the brain as a computer (although it doesn't really resemble a computer, as must be obvious to anyone who has ever worked with computers). The brain does function like a computer in one sense: it stores information in very small pieces, so it can be retrieved in very small pieces. To prove that, look at an example:

Johnny dribbled his basketball while walking to school this morning.

When you've read that sentence, your brain has stored it as a variety of very small ideas, and it has somehow linked those ideas together to reproduce the complete idea stated. To prove that, ask yourself the following questions:

1. Did Johnny go to school this morning?
2. Does Johnny have a basketball?
3. Does Johnny know how to dribble a basketball?
4. Does Johnny live near the school he attends?
5. When was this statement made?

You should be able to answer each of those questions, based on the information given in the example. The answers are:

1. Yes, he did.
2. Yes, he does.
3. Yes, he does.
4. He lives close enough to walk.
5. The statement was made the same day that Johnny walked to school dribbling the basketball.

Now, notice that none of these responses used the whole sentence about Johnny. Your mind was able to draw upon specific pieces of information contained in the original sentence. Each of those pieces of information was stored so that it could be retrieved in response to questions. There are a lot more particles of meaning stored in your mind about that sentence:

1. Johnny is a boy.
2. Johnny is of school age.
3. Johnny is an acquaintance (at least) of the speaker.

Your mind can sort out the information contained in the sentence about Johnny and pass it back to you in any number of different formats. That must mean that your mind has stored the information about Johnny in many different cubbyholes. Each of those cubbyholes contains what we're calling a particle of meaning.

To depart from Johnny for a moment, let's move to something a bit more staid—but helpful: a quote from the seventeenth-century philosopher, René Descartes, translated to modern English:

"The invisible god has created a visible world."

Descartes was the first person to delve into the science of linguistics, the study of how messages are passed from one person to the next. We're not going into the history (or the science) of linguistics; we're just going to borrow Descartes's sentence for an illustration. Descartes's sentence contains many particles of meaning. First, let's extract the obvious ones:

1. There is a god.
2. There is a world.
3. God is invisible.
4. The world is visible.
5. God created the world.
6. The world still exists.
7. God still exists.

Agreed? Certainly Descartes had to have all those pieces of information in his mind to formulate the sentence. You, as a reader, are easily able to extract those same pieces of information in response to questions like "Is God visible?" But there are more particles than the obvious ones:

1. There may be more than one god, but the other gods are not invisible.
2. There may be more than one world, visible or invisible.

And, just as in many communications, the hidden particles are the dangerous ones—the only ones which could have caused mayhem during the seventeenth century. The very implication that there could be more than one god was good for an appearance before the Inquisition in Rome. It is common knowledge what the statement that there might be more than one world did to Galileo.

We'll discuss the importance of particles of meaning further in chapter 2. For right now, though, suffice it to say that they are the keys to messages: the keys to sending messages and the keys to receiving them. In chapter 2, we'll introduce a method of checking for accuracy in business communications based on the extraction of particles of meaning.

Structured Thoughts

Most of us have found ourselves in the following position. We've been asked a question to which we know the answer. It's a subject we haven't thought about for a long time, and we have to do some remembering to retrieve the material. The response goes something like this:

QUESTION: Do you remember there was a guy on TV in the fifties who sang a popular song about a woman who couldn't exactly speak English? It was kind of a sad song and was enormously popular. I can't remember the name of the song or the singer, and it's driving me crazy. Do you know?

RESPONSE: Oh, yeah, I remember. A little guy. Curly hair. Married to Debbie Reynolds. What was his name? Now I remember, he married Elizabeth Taylor. Eddie Fisher, that was his name. The song, I know the one you mean, something about leaving on a train. And there was a son going to college, and a mother talking to him, or a daughter, or something. She spoke broken English; there were a lot of jokes about it. The title sounded like a joke. I remember! "Throw Mama from the Train a Kiss."

Whatever the situation—whether casual or serious—this search-and-retrieve process is familiar to all of us. And the information comes spurting out in small pieces (which are frequently particles of meaning). They don't relate to each other, because we haven't yet found the important particles. So the information comes to the tongue in a line of logic that's only understandable to the speaker. The progression from curly hair to Debbie Reynolds isn't logical; those two pieces of information were simply stored near each other in the brain of the speaker—so they came out together.

Finally, though, the idea coheres. By the end of the search-and-retrieve process, the speaker has finally been able to put together a *structured thought* on the subject. She hasn't made any *grammatical statements* about the song or the singer, but she has found all the information she needs to put together a complete thought with no large blanks in it.

Structured thought is the second milestone on the communication path. It's the point at which you coordinate a series of particles of meaning into a thought that is capable of being intelligible when it's sent. It isn't yet grammatical and is susceptible to many different grammatical forms. Look at the following example:

Structured thought:
EFG Corporation filed a loss for the current year, as it has done for the past three years.

Possible grammatical statements:
1. EFG Corporation filed a loss for the current year, as it has done for the past three years.
2. EFG Corporation filed its fourth straight loss this year.
3. EFG Corporation continued its slump by filing a loss for the fourth year in a row.
4. This year's loss continued EFG Corporation's three-year downward spiral.
5. This year's EFG Corporation loss forged another link in a chain already three years long.

All five of the possible grammatical statements express the same structured thought, but contained in different words and different word orders. That list of five possibilities could have been expanded considerably by adding all the possible permutations of the thought—while keeping the particles of meaning and the structure of the thought intact.

What happens if you skip the structured thought milestone in communication? Easy: gibberish. If a thought isn't structured, it can't be made grammatical, and will make sense only to the sender. The process of putting together structured thoughts is, fortunately, pretty much completely automatic in most of us. The lines below, however, are signals that the process isn't going smoothly, and that the sender needs either more time or more input to communicate properly:

"Give me a minute to get my thoughts together."
"It's right at the tip of my tongue."
"I know that; why can't I remember it?"
"When you asked me, I developed a mental block."

"Isn't it silly that you can't remember things when you need them?"

"I don't quite know how to say this."

Time and deadline pressures frequently cause stoppages in the structured thought process, because they divert energy from the thought process concerning the subject. Instead, all the speaker's energy is directed at the deadline (or the clock). Many students can validate that fact from clock-watching during particularly puzzling examinations. There's a fascination in clocks at times of mental stress. They seem to absorb all the structured thought energy we have at the damndest times.

The concept of structured thoughts is treated at some length in chapters 3 and 4. The problem of sitting down to write is one area of paramount concern to most contemporary business writers. Chapter 3 deals with that bugaboo head-on.

Grammatical Thoughts

Don't let the terminology scare you away. This isn't a discussion of grammar—at least, not in the sense that most of us remember from school. We won't be getting into comma splices, parenthetical phrases, or dangling modifiers. We're going to be working with a concept of grammar much larger than mechanics—and much easier to cope with. If you can read and understand the morning paper or listen to the radio news without puzzling over what's being said—you understand grammar.

Language is composed of two elements: *vocabulary* and *grammar*. Vocabulary gives you the words to use; grammar tells you how to string them together. If you had serious grammar problems, you couldn't order a hamburger at a drive-in, because you wouldn't know what order to put the words in. Consider the following two sentences:

1. Ordinary brown concepts stopped brilliantly behind six goatlike footballs.
2. Six brilliantly stopped brown behind ordinary footballs concepts goatlike.

Notice that both sentences contain the same words, just arranged differently. And let us hasten to add that neither sentence makes sense—at least not to the writers of this book.

These two nonsensical sentences do have a significance, though, despite the fact that they don't make sense. Glance back at them and read them aloud (go ahead, nobody's listening).

Chances are, if you read them aloud, you read sentence one as though it did make sense—as though it were a real sentence. You knew it didn't make sense, but you read it just like it did. Right? The second sentence is a different matter. Chances are that you read it like a string of words, with your voice rising in pitch after each word. That's because you saw no grammar in it. It doesn't read like a sentence, so you didn't treat it like one.

And therein lies the crux of the grammar paradox. The simple fact is: if you speak a language, you are to some extent a master of its grammar—even if you're unaware of that fact. Sentence one is a grammatical statement of a nonthought. Sentence two is a nongrammatical statement of a nonthought. Sentence one isn't gibberish; it is simply nonsense. If you encountered it in a poem, you'd assume it had a meaning that merely wasn't evident to you. No matter where you encountered sentence two, you'd know it was idiocy, that there was no meaning in it.

Every sentence that you formulate has a grammar, a structure that makes each word relate to each other word in such a way that the string of words makes sense. If you've read this far in this book, you probably have no problem whatsoever in this basic English grammar that allows us to communicate, to implement our vocabulary. With that out of the way, let's introduce another concept briefly. That is the concept of media mechanics—the science of comma splices and that sort of thing. It isn't a negligible part of writing, for reasons that will be made obvious later.

Grammatical thoughts are the third milestone on the communication path. Once a structured thought has been made grammatical, it's ready to be communicated, because it's in a form that allows it to be spoken or written. Don't let anyone kid you about grammar. There's no way to describe it fully—and there are virtually no hard-and-fast rules to it. It's entirely flexible, within some definitions. You know the boundaries set by those definitions, because you know when something said to you doesn't make sense.

Medium

Now we come to the birth of a transmittable message: putting it into a medium. That medium may be speech; it may be writing on paper; it may be talking on the telephone; it may be sign language. There are any number of possible media for a message—and each different medium has its own characteristics and problems. We'll deal primarily with two: speech and writing. When we write about speech, we'll be writing about face-to-face encounters, which means two-way communication. When we write about writing, we'll tackle the more complex problem of one-way communication with no immediate feedback.

The most important thing to remember about a medium is that it should be absolutely neutral. It should neither add to nor detract from the message. It should merely be a receptacle that carries meaning from one person to another—and, as such, it should be relatively easy to handle. As most of us know, however, things aren't always as they should be, and media do give us problems from time to time.

Chapters 6, 7, 8, and 9 deal with handling specific media: letters and memoranda, reports, committee-generated documents, and oral presentations. These four are the media most commonly and most critically encountered in the business world. If you master these, you can handle any other communication problem you might come up against.

Perception

The three steps on the perception side of the communication path are a reversal of the three steps that precede the medium. The receiver of a message perceives a grammatical thought, extracts meaning from it, and stores meaning for future use. We'll discuss the all-important topic of reading for meaning in chapter 10. Although we maintain for certain practical purposes that miscommunication is the fault of the sender of a message, we realize the extreme importance of intelligent perception. It almost follows automatically (fortunately) that if you send messages correctly, you'll receive messages comparatively well. In chapter 10, we'll provide some assists over the rough spots.

Pulling It All Together

When a quarterback throws a long pass to a running end in a football game, he aims not for where the runner is, but for where he will be when the pass gets to him. That same judgment is called for in using and benefiting from the communication path we have set up. The more you know about your reader, and the more you gear your communication specifically to your reader, the more likely you are to succeed in getting your message across. We'll discuss evaluating your own writing in chapter 11— evaluating it in terms of how well it communicates. Are your messages received correctly most of the time? How many times do people write back to ask you for clarification? How often do you wait for a response to a letter or memo—and that response never comes or comes back wrong?

This is a very nuts-and-bolts kind of book. Our suggestions

are practical and everyday; they aren't intended to be high-flown and theoretical. What business needs today is not more theory about communication. It just needs better quality in speaking and writing—plain and simple. The losses to business each year because of poor communication are staggering. Look at your own situation. If paperwork were always done right the first time, if every memo and every letter got results—how much faster and easier would life be? That "fast and easy" translates into money in business. It allows businesses to operate with more efficient, smaller staffs. More time for innovation, less need for paper-sustained bureaucracy.

We think you'll find the chapters ahead helpful and interesting. Some of the suggestions we make should be helpful even if you're already an able communicator. Our basic feeling about communications is that the field has been cluttered over the past few years—cluttered by a lot of talk and by fast-paced innovation in communication hardware. Some people are fooled into thinking that if they use pretty slides, their oral presentations are more effective; that if their letters are typed by a computer operator in a word processing center, those letters make better sense. These are misconceptions. We're here to provide some shirt-sleeve answers that may help.

Exercises

1. Compare the time and cost of sending a memo to someone in another department with calling them by phone and with seeing them in person.
2. In each case in problem 1, identify the most expensive and time consuming part of the communication path.

Discuss, in each of the examples in exercises 3 through 6, how the receiver would understand less, understand something different, and understand more.

3. "I have assigned chapters 1–5. The test next Tuesday will cover chapters 1–7."
4. To: Isabel Leath
    From: Marry Nolte
    Subject: Error in book order
    This is our second note on the errors we have found in the latest shipment of books. The book Rowing for Fun is printed in paper and hardback. We received 12 hard and 16 paper and were billed $383.73. We ordered 2 hard and 26 paper. I would appreciate some action on this problem.
5. The mechanic tells you over the telephone that your car

won't be ready until 6:00 P.M. instead of 4:30 P.M.

6. A newspaper headline: "Governor Attacks Legislature on Taxes."

In each of exercises 7 through 10, identify the basic particles of meaning.

7. Raymond removed three dollars from his mother's purse and purchased several packs of bubble gum with baseball cards.

8. After three years as supervisor of word processing, Wanda Lundy was promoted to manager of office systems.

9. Corporate profits rose 20 percent over the previous year even though sales only increased 2 percent.

10. The corporation is a defendant in numerous lawsuits in which it is not covered by insurance. It is not anticipated that these suits will result in payments that would affect net assets.

In each of exercises 11 through 15, a structured thought is provided. Develop three possible grammatical statements for each.

11. The company has seen an increase of 40 percent in class-action suits and a continuation of several antitrust actions for the third year in a row.

12. We propose staffing increase from twenty-eight to thirty-seven people to accommodate additional workload generated by the recharging method.

13. Eugene Smith found a job in a liquor store as a clerk after interviewing for three other clerical jobs.

14. The Supreme Court decided the Saxon case in favor of the plaintiff after meeting for neary three hours in the last session.

15. The chairs you ordered a month ago will not be in for two months due to a clerical error.

16. Since you have been in your current job, you have probably received a number of memos that use shorthand and jargon. Pull out two of these memos. What would someone new to the job do? How long would it take to decipher this? What are the prices for errors?

2
The Meaning Itself

n its most elemental form, language is composed entirely of separate and distinct particles of meaning. Although Tarzan's one-liner, "me Tarzan, you Jane," has become a byword for the inarticulate, it is a good example of direct, totally simplified language.[1] Based on Tarzan's statement, it would be possible for Jane to answer several questions:

1. "Who am I?"   (answer: Jane)
2. "Who are you?"   (answer: Tarzan)
3. "Who is Tarzan?"   (answer: you)
4. "Who is Jane?"   (answer: me).

There you have perfect economy of language: the answers to four questions in a four-word sentence. It does leave something to be desired in terms of elegance. The grammarian would point out that it lacks verbs; the semanticist would tell you it relies on gesture for meaning. It is emphatically a spoken message rather than a written one.

This type of language—absolutely direct, devoid of grammar or ornament of any kind—is common in some spoken situations. A tourist who does not speak the native language is reduced to similar statements, accompanied by descriptive gestures. An adult, speaking to a very small child, adopts a drastically curtailed version of the language. A man who needs the glycerine capsules in the vest pocket of his suit may well gasp "Pills! Pocket!"—and get his meaning across perfectly well.

Usually, though, this ungrammatical language, this use of

---

1. *We don't intend to imply that primitive languages (Hollywood notwith-standing) are simple. In fact, they're usually far more grammatically complex than most modern languages.*

particles of meaning without the structure of language, is accompanied by gesticulation of some sort. Tarzan taps his own chest to identify Tarzan; he points at the beautiful girl to identify Jane. The tourist who needs street directions looks puzzled and points to her map while saying "Me. Hotel. Go." When a situation not easily pantomimed arises, this direct system of language fails. It also fails in written language, which lacks the immediacy of spoken language and can't rely on body language or facial expression for help. Because of that, the style is seldom used other than for emergencies, or predicaments in which no other language is available. After all, language has a lot more to offer than "me Tarzan, you Jane."

Identifying Particles of Meaning

We discussed particles of meaning briefly in the first chapter, illustrating them with Descartes's sentence about an invisible god who created a visible world. It is possible to extract a list of particles from any grammatical sentence:[2]

1. Our aluminum extruding division increased sales by 35 percent during the past year.
   a. We have more than one division.
   b. One of them extrudes aluminum.
   c. It is a division which sells its products.
   d. It increased its sales.
   e. The amount of the increase is 35 percent.
   f. The time period is the year past.
2. We won't be needing you here anymore after June 1.
   a. We need you now.
   b. We will not need you after June 1.
   c. You are not to come to work after June 1.
   d. You will not be paid after June 1.

The particles of meaning that can be extracted from any rational sentence are nothing more or less than a catalogue of the ideas that the sentence communicates. Some ideas are stated (1b, 1d, 1e, 1f, 2b); others are clearly implied (1a, 1c, 2a, 2c, 2d). A reasonable and careful reader will be able to understand all of them with little effort. More important, that reader should be able to respond to questions concerning each of them—indicating that each piece of information is stored independently of the others in the mind of the receiver.

---

2. *Nongrammatical sentences are a different matter, because the relationships between words are left vague or unstated.*

Transferral and Storage of Particles

The ability to communicate ideas is one of the faculties that separates man from beast. The more you try to define that faculty, the deeper you dig into a hole of exceptions, additions, generalities, and language inadequacies. Suffice it to say, the ability to transfer meaning from one person to another rests in the ability to generate and to understand language (that is, to speak and listen, to write and read).

We transfer ideas by means of language, which is an agreed upon set of arbitrary symbols. Languages come in all manner of forms; ethnic or national languages (such as English, French, Russian, Urdu) are only one category. Most people are multilingual—that is, they speak several languages (or at least understand several). There probably isn't a reader of this book who doesn't consider himself fluent in several of the following:

a national language
numbers (mathematics)
musical notation
chemical notation
FORTRAN or COBOL
graphics (arrows, street signs, for example)
sign language (Franslan, Ameslan)
gesture (body language)
pictures

And there are more. But each of these languages is a set of agreed upon symbols—and each transcends the others in some way. An English musician and a Russian musician both see the same meaning in:

Minuet in G major, J. S. Bach, from the notebook of Anna Magdalena Bach.

They see the first four bars of a Bach minuet. Nevertheless, there's nothing inherent in the marks on the paper that must mean a certain series of pitches and a certain rhythm. It is only that musical language is universally agreed upon.

Similarly, a deaf French scientist whose primary language is Franslan can easily communicate an idea to a Japanese engineer with a symbol like the following:

$$CH_3OH$$

although there's nothing to indicate to the laity that those letters mean anything but gibberish. (To the French scientist and the Japanese engineer, they denote methyl alcohol.)

It's rules that allow language to function as a transmitter of ideas and information. If you don't understand the rules of musical notation, you can't read Bach's minuet—despite the fact that a popular song plagiarizes it note for note. If you don't know that C is carbon, that H is hydrogen, and that O is oxygen—you can't possibly understand that CH_3OH is the compound you use to sterilize a thermometer before you stick it in your mouth. What if the rules are violated? What if one scientist decided to represent carbon by a K? No one would recognize KH_3OH as anything.

This whole discussion may seem painfully obvious (or worse, academic), but it has a point. The whole—the only—use of language depends on its having rules. And when the rules are abandoned, language ceases to exist.

Communication is wholly dependent on a strict observance of the rules of language. We'll discuss this at length later; for now, it's important to realize that the midpoint in the communication path (the medium) becomes an insurmountable obstacle without those troublesome rules.

When language is properly used and communication takes place, the receiver of a message must break it down and store it—in particles of meaning. The process of storage is the only segment of the communication path that is entirely unseen and unseeable by the sender. It is the point at which communication (in some form) has taken place, whether correct or incorrect. The only way to test for correctness is to monitor whatever feedback is available. Consider the following case study.

Tom Weatherly is the manager of an office building with a very high occupancy rate. The parking facilities at the building are adequate to current needs. Weatherly, with an eye to the future, anticipates the day when construction of a new building next door will be a profitable investment. He writes to the owner of the building, Myron Jones:

To: Myron Jones, Owner
From: Tom Weatherly, Building Manager
Subject: Parking Lot at Fourth and Pine

As you know there is a fifty-car parking lot located next to your building near the corner of Fourth and Pine. I have recently heard that the owner, Herbert Farnsworth, passed away. His widow, Melba Farnsworth, is interested in selling. Your building is currently 90 percent occupied. Please advise if you wish me to take further action.

Weatherly has tried to convey the following particles of meaning to Jones:

1. There is a fifty-car lot next door.
2. It is available for purchase.
3. It would be a good purchase for future expansion of office space (implied).

He receives back the following memorandum from Myron Jones:

To: Tom Weatherly, Building Manager
From: Myron Jones, Owner
Subject: Your Memo on the Parking Lot at Fourth and Pine

I have received your memorandum and reviewed the opportunity. My understanding is that our current parking lot is of sufficient size. Funds are not available for the low priority of an additional parking lot.

Clearly, something is amiss. Jones has responded to a suggestion on a basis that Tom Weatherly never intended to imply. Weatherly never considered suggesting the acquisition of the parking lot as a parking lot—but as a hedge against future needs for more office space.

It's easy to see where the message went awry. There was no reason for Jones to see the suggestion as anything more than a parking lot acquisition. And, being a busy man, he responded to the suggestion that he saw at a first reading. After all, does a short memo usually require more than one reading? Jones read the memo, and extracted the following particles of meaning:

1. There is a fifty-car lot next door.
2. It is available for purchase.
3. If purchased, it would provide additional (unnecessary) parking facilities.

That message wasn't what was intended, but that was what got through. And Weatherly only found that out when he received Jones's response (feedback). Now that he sees what has transpired, he can try to remedy the situation, but he has to face the following hurdles which weren't there before:

1. Time has been lost.
2. A decision has been made.

To pursue the proposition further, Weatherly has either to admit writing a poor letter or to imply that Jones didn't read carefully (either "I guess I didn't say what I meant" or "You didn't understand what I meant"). Neither course is particularly attractive.

Using Particles of Meaning

There's a thread through the maze of communication. There's a method by which a communicator can reasonably ensure that his message will get across accurately. That thread is the meaning itself. Too often, the meaning gets extremely short shrift in the speaking-writing process.

The usual pattern in communicating is something like this. You decide what you want to say (mentally, with no notes on paper), then you write it down and mail it. It's a simple process. Some folks (usually those with secretaries) reread their missives for typographical errors, punctuation errors, and such before mailing them. But by the time a letter is typed and an envelope addressed, the meaning has usually gone out of the mind of the sender. She's trapped in the language—trapped between admiration of her prose and inspection of the secretary's grammar skills. There's no established method for checking letters for accuracy of meaning. You read through it, you sign it, you mail it—and you hope for the best.

That pattern usually isn't followed in the alternate language forms (mathematics, chemistry, music, COBOL, and others). Virtually no one reads a federal income tax form solely for grammatical and typing accuracy. It's read for meaning—for accuracy and clarity. Consider the following example.

A Mathematical Error

You are getting ready to go on vacation, and you want to pay off your credit card account so you won't be in arrears when you return next month. You've saved your charge slips and can see that the total amount you have charged is $347. You know that the interest rate on your card is 18 percent per annum, which is equal to 1.5 percent monthly. You need to calculate the interest you have incurred, add it to your balance, and pay the total. You multiply it out:

$347   (charges made)
×1.015   (balance + interest)
1735
347
347
399.05 = $399.05 (current balance)

What do you do next? Write a check and mail it? No. You check your multiplication, and you find that you made an error—that the problem should actually read like this:

$347   (charges made)
×1.015   (balance + interest)
1735
347   (correct decimal placement)
347
352.205 = $352.21 (current balance)

After checking again to see if you made another error, you'd pay the second (correct) balance.

What happened? You made an error in meaning, you located it—automatically—and you corrected it before sending it out. There are two reasons for the checking you did:

1. Money is intrinsically important—and therefore worth checking.
2. Mathematical language is easy to check.

Unfortunately, no quick and easy method exists for the same kind of check on the accuracy of written prose (national languages). And, because there is no easy method of checking, messages usually aren't checked for accuracy of meaning. They're checked for the easy things—grammar, punctuation, spelling. And it's assumed that the meaning will follow. Not true.

We need to develop a method of checking message accuracy—an easy, almost mechanical method. And that's where our discussion of particles of meaning becomes utilitarian, rather than merely theoretical.

The Communication Path Reexamined

Take another look at the communication path on page 5. Note that we begin and end with the same entry: particles of meaning. We've agreed that a successful message is one in which the particles of meaning at both ends of the path are identical. For now, let's consider the only objective of communication as: to move the particles of meaning from one mind to another absolutely intact. We'll monitor the process like this:

1. Make a list of particles to be conveyed.
2. Structure a message logically (outline or simple notes).
3. Check to be sure that the particles still survive.
4. Compose a letter.
5. Check to be sure that the particles still survive.
6. Mail it, requesting a response.
7. Check the response to be sure that the particles still survive.
If they do, then the message was successful.

Here's a situation: Marie Collins, a long-range planning analyst for a fast-food chain, has seen the following ad in the *Wall Street Journal*'s "Mart" section under "Positions Available."

Administrative Director
The Northern Region of the nation's largest firm in franchise staff training is in search of an Administrative Director. Applicants should have franchise management experience, be strong in public relations, and possess leadership ability. This position offers challenge and opportunity for advancement to a top quality, motivated, and success-oriented person. Salary open. Outstanding fringe benefits. Profit sharing available. Respond to WSJ 22D-348.

She has decided to submit a letter of application to this "blind" ad. She underlines the areas of the ad she has selected to emphasize in her reply:

Administrative Director
The Northern Region of the nation's largest firm in <u>franchise staff training</u> is in search of an Administrative Director. Applicants should have <u>franchise management experience</u>, be strong in <u>public relations</u>, and possess <u>leadership ability</u>. This position offers challenge and opportunity for advancement to a top quality, motivated, and <u>success-oriented</u> person. Salary open. Outstanding fringe benefits. Profit sharing available. Respond to WSJ 22D-348.

Collins has been in her current position for three years (where she reports directly to an executive vice-president). Her previous experience includes work in the advertising department of another franchise operation—that one in dry cleaning. In her previous position, she held frequent seminars for members of the sales staff on matters such as sales and business projection techniques. She decides on the following particles of meaning for her letter. That is, she wants to convey most strongly the following ideas:

1. familiarity with franchise operations
2. advertising experience related to public relations
3. seminar experience as a form of staff training
4. recent experience in top management reporting situation
5. innovativeness
6. eagerness for a "mid-career change" to increase chances for brighter future

With this list of particles in mind, she drafts a letter:

Dear Sir:

This letter is in response to your advertisement for an Administrative Director. I have enclosed my resume for your consideration.

I have been in my present position for three years. While I like the job, I feel that I have gone as far as I can with the firm.
As you can see from my resume, I have substantial experience in franchising—both in dry cleaning and in fast foods. In addition, I have conducted more than ten in-plant seminars, all of which were well received.

My experience in franchising is current and extensive. It includes all phases of the business, from advertising to operations.
I hope to hear from you.

Very truly yours,
M. O. Collins

It's a reasonably good letter. Replying to an ad of this type is always difficult; one doesn't know what company is advertising. But let's see how well Marie's original list of ideas (particles of meaning) survived her first draft. She certainly hit point one with sufficient clout, as well as number three. There's some doubt about how well she covered the others. She did mention her advertising experience (which shows on her resume as well), but didn't relate it back to the code words in the ad ("public relations"). She did not emphasize her top management reporting position, except on her resume. She totally omitted her innovative character. Worst of all, she turned item number six into a negative idea, rather than a positive one.

Marie might assume that her resume will speak for itself in the areas she omitted or glossed over. And it might. But Marie's cover letter will speak first—and it will guide the reader's perception of her resume. If she tells him to look for top management experience, he will; if she doesn't, he may not. If she doesn't make the connection between public relations and advertising, he may not either. And, most important, he may see her as a malcontent, rather than as the ambitious person she is, if she doesn't change the tone of her comments about having gone about as far as she can.

Having checked for the survival of her list of particles of meaning, Marie revises her letter:

Dear Sir:

This letter is in response to your advertisement for an Administrative Director. I have enclosed my resume for your consideration.

As the resume indicates, I have a varied background in franchising—all of it up-to-date and current. My work in the advertising department of XYZ Dry Cleaning Sales, Inc. gave me a familiarity with public relations which I have been able to build on since then. The seminars I conducted during my time at XYZ gave me a good handle on staff training and the problems associated with it.

Since I joined ABC Fast Foods three years ago, I've been working on ABC's closely held long-range plan—and have developed several concepts on my own that have begun to blossom over the past few months.

I've invested most of my working life thus far in the franchising business, and I think I'm ready for a responsible position such as the one you've advertised. I'm no job-hopper, as you can plainly see from my resume. But new opportunities beckon with broader horizons; a chance for my experience to work for me—and for you. I hope to hear from you.

Very truly yours,
Marie Collins

Without comparing the second draft to the first, compare it to the list of particles to be conveyed. They're all there, and in a form that will be easily understood by the reader. There are references to specifics in the resume, which will help the reader understand it—a document notorious for its dullness and lack of proper emphasis.[4] Her attitude is well depicted, and she has decided not to hide behind the asexual "M. O. Collins." Marie has a good chance of at least having her resume considered.

Particles of Meaning as Quality Control

When you're working with mathematics or chemistry, you've got a clear set of information to work with. You can identify correct and incorrect processes because the rules are so clear and so inflexible. A checking device for writing has to come as close as possible to that clarity. A list of particles of meaning is such a device. If you take the extra time (it isn't much) to work with a list of particles for your important letters and reports, you'll find the added quality control improves your performance. If you never lose sight of your particles of meaning—if they're your guide through your own prose—you won't run much risk of being misunderstood.

To function as a quality controller, your list of particles of meaning has to be written—and written simply. Don't trust yourself to keep it all in your head. A checking device that has no head start on the process it's checking is no checking device at all.

Two Kinds of Particles

As you've probably already noticed, we've been working so far with two very different kinds of particles of meaning. In the first chapter, we analyzed a sentence for all the segments of meaning contained within it—all of them—and we came out with a list of meanings much longer than the sentence itself. Those particles

---

4. *Face facts. Resumes are dull reading and only really tell your story to you. Without a guide to the highlights, your potential employer will fall asleep between the dates, addresses, names, and titles. Give him an idea of what you're like, so he'll know he's reading about a person, not a cipher. (See the Special Section, "Using Communication Skills to Get a Job," for further discussion.)*

are *sentence-level particles*. We'll use sentence-level particles quite heavily in chapter 5, "Decisions, Decisions."

The particles we've been working with during our case study of Marie Collins are *storage-level particles*. These are the particles of meaning you want to transfer more than all others, the particles of a message you want the reader to be able to store and retrieve with greatest ease. Your list of storage-level particles represents the guts of your communication. If one of these is missed, amplified out of perspective, or improperly deemphasized, your message is a failure.

To clarify the distinction between the two levels, consider the following:

> We must dare to think "unthinkable" thoughts. We must learn to explore all the options and possibilities that confront us in a complex and rapidly changing world. We must learn to welcome and not to fear the voices of dissent. We must dare to think about "unthinkable things" because when things become unthinkable, thinking stops and action becomes mindless.[5]

An exhaustive catalog of sentence-level particles in Senator Fulbright's message would be extremely lengthy, but might start off like this:

1. Some thoughts are unthinkable.
2. We can avoid thinking about them.
3. We can think about them.
4. We should think about them.
5. It is necessary that we think about them.
6. The world is changing.
7. The world is changing rapidly.
8. The world is complex.
9. We can avoid learning about the world.
10. We can learn about the world.
11. We should learn about the world.
12. It is necessary that we learn about the world.
13. The world contains options.
14. The world contains possibilities.

. . . And so on. And that list doesn't even get us fully through the

---

5. *From a speech in the U.S. Senate, 27 March 1964, by Senator James William Fulbright (U.S., Congress, Senate,* Congressional Record *110, no. 4: 252–254).*

second sentence. A complete list, carefully compiled, might go on for pages. But the speaker wasn't concerned that we absorb and remember all these sentence-level particles. He was concerned that certain important thoughts be conveyed strongly:

1. We must dare to think "unthinkable" thoughts.
2. If we don't, we will be mindless in our actions.

These two thoughts are storage-level particles. They're the essence of Senator Fulbright's message to the Senate. They're unelaborated, but they're a distillation of the paragraph. If we miss those two thoughts, then the paragraph has failed to communicate with us.

Failure to Communicate

Any time a storage-level particle is missed in communication, the message is to some extent a failure. The more important the missed particle, the more massive the failure. There are several common errors that cause such failures. The most common is simple omission. Marie Collins, our mythical long-range planner, simply deleted her innovative character from her particle list in the process of transferring the list to her first draft.

The second most common error is presumption. Marie, for instance, presumed that the reader would read and understand her resume, distilling from it her top management reporting position. Presumption is a cardinal sin in communicating, but one that's both insidious and attractive. Writers frequently appear to themselves to overstate their cases. Why? As a writer, you have a body of knowledge and associations that make up your mental environment. You've lived with them for a long time; they've become such an integral part of you that you begin to take for granted that others have the same (or similar) knowledge. Having taken that for granted, you communicate on that basis (or don't communicate, as a frequent result). Here's an example familiar to all of us.

> You are trying to explain your job to someone—your spouse, a friend, a new colleague. You're forced to repeat yourself constantly, because your vocabulary is filled with references totally unknown to your listener. You find yourself saying things like, "I know I told you about the Stillheimer case, because I remember telling you that I ran into Mary Franciscus in Chicago and she was working on the same case." A dim light goes on in the listener's face, but the train of

thought before the "Franciscus" interruption has been broken and has to be reestablished.

Presumption is a dangerous communication vice, because listeners and readers often don't respond to it at all. They nod at you just like they knew what you were talking about—and promptly forget the whole conversation (just like they forgot about the Stillheimer case in the first place).

Common examples of presumption include use of technical references that aren't widely known or understood, use of jargon, and use of personal references. Compare the two following quotations from the poet Ezra Pound:

1. And the betrayers of language
   . . . . n and the press gang
   And those who had lied for hire;
   The perverts, the perverters of language, the perverts,
       who have set money-lust
   Before the pleasures of the senses;
   howling, as of a hen-yard in a printinghouse, the clatter
       of presses,
   the blowing of dry dust and stray paper,
   foetor, sweat, the stench of stale oranges.[6]

2. Literature is news that stays news.

The first quotation is somewhat unintelligible, is it not? who knows who ". . . . n" is? Who knows that "foetor" is a strong, offensive smell? Without a guidebook or a lot of footnotes, the passage is gobbledygook. Why? Because the poet has chosen references that are oblique, personal, hidden. The passsage doesn't communicate much to the person who doesn't choose to study it carefully.[7] The second quotation hardly seems to have flown from the same man's pen. But it did. It speaks directly, says what it has to say, and stops.

The point of this discussion is that the presumption allowed the poet (because some people will always stop to research the footnotes, as Pound well knew) is simply not allowed the rest of us. And when Pound wanted to write to a wide audience, he relinquished his poetic license, and talked straight.

---

6.   The Cantos of Ezra Pound Copyright © 1934 by Ezra Pound. Reprinted by permission of New Directions.

7.   Not to mention the fact the passage has no verb and, therefore, no coherent grammar. Ah, poetry!

The third common cause of failure to communicate is lack of proper emphasis. If an important storage-level particle is sandwiched between unimportant particles, it may well be missed by the reader. In this regard, remember that *first* and *last* are the most emphatic positions in a message. Look back at the paragraph from Senator Fulbright. The two storage-level particles in the paragraph appear as the beginning and closing sentences. The prevalent theory of sandwiching a piece of bad news between two compliments is risky at best. The reader or listener may miss the bad news completely; alternatively, he may be annoyed by the cloying quality of your sandwich bread.

Start off with what you mean to say. Then say it, and be done with it. Say it simply (but elegantly) and in words that your audience will understand. You can't miss.

The Message Itself

The backbone of any successful communication must be the information you want to get across. If you're ordering a new Jaguar, and you want the red one, you don't call the dealer and say, "Listen, I don't want yellow or green or black or white or tan or grey or blue." You say, "I want the red one." It's the same for any message. The message itself must organize your communication. Your message must be a vehicle for the thought you're conveying. That means that you must structure your letter, your report, your presentation—solely to communicate your message. Everything else you do must in some way enhance that primary aim.

Your list of storage-level particles must remain intact throughout your communication. It must survive the pitfalls of deletion, presumption, and lack of emphasis. It must survive your own admiration (or fear) of your writing style. If you read a draft of a letter and find that some particles are missing, *throw it away.* Start over from scratch, with a blank piece of paper. Don't attempt to improve a draft that is missing important particles. The best you can do is a piece of patchwork, frequently an unattractive piece that lacks transitions, logic, flow. Your first draft must contain all the information you want. Let the form of the message be dictated by the message itself. Anything else is wrong.

The idea of pitching a draft may be uncomfortable to you, but it's the only practical approach to the job. You wouldn't accept a budget forecast that made no allowance for personnel. You wouldn't allow it to be patched together with some new entries—because you would know that the thinking behind it was faulty enough to delete an all-important concept. You'd want the budget group to start over. Follow the same precept in your writing. No matter how polished your prose, no matter how you admire your language or your approach—refuse to work with a draft that is incomplete in terms of particles. It can only lead to failure.

To get that complete draft, we'll propose a method of sitting down to write that will facilitate your achieving a complete list of storage-level particles. Coming right up, in chapter 3.

Exercises

In each of exercises 1 through 6, identify the sentence-level particles of meaning.

1. To: Rhonda White
    From: Sylvia Wahl
    Subject: Expense Reports
    The last three travel expense reports you submitted have had errors that could have been avoided by following proper procedures. One error relates to mileage calculations. Reimbursement is at the rate of 17¢ per mile, not 15¢. For airport parking we must have receipts.
2. Bobby has excellent potential as a student. His work in mathematics and spelling has improved since class began.
3. "Joe, I talked to William Harvey about the payroll problem. If they could use the proper FDA form, they would have their problems solved. Could you tell them to read the FDA form's procedures?"
4. The island of Lawai is situated only 100 miles from Hana airport. The average temperature is 74°. Average rainfall is only 15 inches per year. The island is a green, verdant paradise.
5. (*At bottom of menu*) "Minimum service charge per person is $1.00."
6. The company has experienced problems due to three recall campaigns. The latest one involves over 400,000 cars. Industrywide, more cars were recalled than made in 1977.
7. For each of problems 1 through 6, identify the storage-level particles.
8. Identify several language terms that you use in your job frequently. Do they take on various meanings?

In each of the examples in exercises 9 through 11, you are given the particles and the body of a memo intended to convey them. Discuss what is wrong with the memo.

9. a. I have a 1976 Ford Sedan.
   b. Your agency tried to fix the idling speed.
   c. The idling speed still doesn't work.
   d. Your agency should fix it—now.
   I have had my car in several times to be fixed by your mechanics. They apparently can't fix it right. This problem has caused me a lot of inconvenience. The idling speed still doesn't work. When are you going to fix it?
10. a. Bob Russell has been a good performer.
    b. Bob is always on time.
    c. Bob needs managerial training.
    d. Bob can improve and move into management.
    I have just completed a review of Bob Russell's performance over the past year. He is always at the office on time. He performs his job well. Bob, however, does need managerial training to be eligible for promotion.
11. a. The radio has three knobs.
    b. The knob on the left is volume.
    c. The knob in the middle is station tuning.
    d. The knob on the right is for tone.
    This manual describes the way to use instant radio set. With a little practice you will easily enjoy. There are three dials. One dial is for volume—turn it to the right for higher volume. The second knob is for tone. The other knob is for station tuning to adjust the station control.

EMO: _____

Part 2
Structuring Your Thoughts

3
Sitting Down to Write

Imagine that you have to put together a summary activity report on your current projects for your new vice-president. She's a go-getter; she wants this report today. You're anxious to make a good impression (and to keep your projects funded), so you want to put your best effort into this report.

What happens? You sit down with a yellow pad and a pencil, and you stare at them. You're currently working on three seemingly unrelated ideas, but you know that down the road a bit they're going to come together into a single proposal for a new product line. You're not nearly ready to say that, though. You've no shortage of information. What you lack in this situation is the structure that will allow you to illuminate your particles of meaning through intelligible, precise words.

So you stare and you fidget, waiting for the first paragraph— or the first word—to write itself down and give you a lead-in to the material. You have no models to base this report on.

Traditional wisdom dictates that you just start writing, just put something down, and worry later about how it sounds. Get into it, and your problems will decrease. Then you can revise your opening after you've finished the piece—the report, the letter, the press release. But it's easier said than done, and it's dangerous, because you might start off in the wrong direction, and your first thought inevitably leads to your second thought, then to your third, and so on. By the time you've finished, you've said something entirely different from what you intended to say.

Writing sometimes seems to have a life and a will of its own. You aren't easily led astray in speech by your own eloquence, because you're accustomed to the sound of your voice, the extent of your vocabulary, and the normal structure of your comments. Not so with writing. Because writing is unfamiliar, it tends to be a more difficult task to write in a straight line. It's much like speaking a foreign language; you say what you know how to say, not what you mean to say—your skills and your vocabulary shape your ideas, instead of the reverse.

It's not at all unusual, for instance, to reach a conclusion in writing that you would never have considered in speech. The act of writing pushes you in directions you have no way of anticipating. The medium begins to warp the message. And that's dangerous. Communication should be a tool to convey information, not to modify it.

Many of us were taught in school to make outlines before we wrote. Most of us gave up making outlines as soon as we weren't required to show them on our exams. The reason is simple: to make an outline, you still have to figure out where to start. And once you've figured out where to start, who needs an outline?

Why Is Starting a Problem?

In the first place, many people are used to having problems sitting down to write, so they expect them. When you expect problems, problems have a way of materializing. If you always have a problem sitting down to write, and you don't do anything to get rid of it—you're going to keep having it.

The coffee and cigarettes routine is a frequent crutch. Why? You probably developed the habit during college, and you've never dropped it. Maybe it helps get those barriers to come a-tumblin' down, maybe it doesn't. Maybe you don't smoke and don't drink coffee, so you have other little things you do (go to the bathroom, stretch, sharpen your sixteen pencils, clear your desk). It all adds up to the same thing: you're trying to re-create a situation in the past when you were able to write.

Superstition takes hold of us at the most surprising times. If you sat facing a particular wall the last time you wrote a report, you may find yourself turning your typewriter around to face that wall the next time. These superstitions take the form of statements like "I always do my best writing between eight and ten in the morning," "I always write with a pencil," "I can't write on unlined paper," or "I have to have quiet, or I can't think." The nonsense of statements like these is accepted as part of life, despite the obviously ludicrous logic. You'd never say the same things about talking. Nobody, for instance, does his best talking between eight and ten in the morning; very few people have to have absolute quiet to think while they talk. People who can hear a pin drop when they're composing a memo can shout over an unbelievable din at a cocktail party without giving it a second thought. Why? You talk English, and you write English—are the two not the same?

No, they are not the same. Everybody knows that, and we're not going to try to tell you otherwise. But the differences aren't the ones you might expect. The spoken language and the written language are different, it's true, but not so very different that problems should arise. You can say things you'd never write for a variety of reasons—but they're not the reasons you have trouble writing.

You have trouble writing because you don't spend much of your life doing it. You probably didn't learn to read and write until you were five or six years old; at that point you were already quite fluent in the spoken language. And you probably didn't start communicating in writing until much later (answering questions on a test isn't communicating; neither is writing a form thank-you letter to Aunt Sarah after Christmas). Some people never learn to communicate by writing; they learn instead to be tested by writing. That's a by-product of our educational system (the only time you write is when the teacher is going to grade you on it). If you feel your reputation is on the line every time you pick up a pen, you're probably suffering from a testing syndrome—and you probably didn't test too well as a student.

But even if you have learned to communicate by writing, it's a little-used skill when compared to others, such as talking. We are simply not writing-oriented people in a speaking civilization. When was the last time you had a dream in which people wrote to communicate? Silly question, isn't it? People don't write in dreams, they talk. We're all accustomed to talking, and very few of us are accustomed to writing.

So what's the answer? Write more? It would probably help, but nobody has the time or the inclination. No, the answer isn't writing more; it's paying more attention to the demands that writing makes on us.

From Brain to Mouth

Somebody asks you a question. You know the answer, so you speak.

QUESTION: What color is your tie?
ANSWER: Blue.

Simple. There was no conscious shaping of an answer; you just

opened your mouth, and the sounds came out, like they always
do. Now try the same situation in writing.

Memorandum
Date: 23 August 1977
To: Harold Smith
From: Jeanette Walton
Subject: Tie Color

What color is your tie?

You know what color your tie is: it's blue. How do you phrase your
reply? "Dear Jeanette: Blue." Probably not. Even if you decide
on such a direct course of reply, you have questions to answer
("Should I put a period after the word *blue* even though it's not a
sentence?" "Will Jeanette know what I'm talking about if I write a
one-word reply?"). The situation becomes more complicated. You
have to find a memo form, a pen or pencil, an envelope, and you
probably have to explain yourself.

Memorandum
Date: 24 August 1977
To: Jeanette Walton
From: Harold Smith
Subject: Tie Color/23 August

In response to your question, I wore a blue tie yesterday. I'm
wearing a red tie today. Thanks.
(signed)
Harold

It's not hard to see why writing is a more difficult form of
communication, just in terms of logistics. More important, it's a
much more conscious process than speaking. Your mind sends
messages through your mouth very easily. You have no trouble
forming words or sentences in normal speech. You accompany
them with whatever gestures you care to use, but you don't
have to think to talk (the truth of that statement is everywhere
apparent). You do have to think to write.

   The linkup between your brain and your hand is much more
difficult to establish than the more customary brain-to-mouth
one. As a society, we simply aren't accustomed to expressing
our thoughts with our pens in our hands. It's not surprising,
therefore, that we have some amount of trouble doing so. Nor is it
surprising that we often try to find a way around the problem

instead of facing it. The most common substitute for this linkup is translation of speech into writing. The harrassed business-person formulates a letter orally (either to herself or by dictation to a secretary), and then commits it to writing. This procedure, although commonly followed, has severe limitations. Most people have a working vocabulary in speech considerably smaller and less emphatic than the one they command in writing. Why? Because speech is almost always reinforced by nonverbal communication, or by repetition, tone of voice, and so on. When speech is translated into writing, it frequently ends up unem-phatic or, worse, puzzling.

The system of translation effectively adds another step to the communication path, by breaking the medium into two cate-gories. And, as any problem solver knows, the addition of an extra step provides additional margin for error. The best system in communication, as in other disciplines, is the simplest system. The prevalent suggestion that we should "write more like we talk" is culpable in this problem area.

It's true that we ought to "write more like we talk" in certain ways. Writing should be natural, unstuffy, direct, simple, and straightforward—like speech. But it requires a different set of media rules, and speech translated into writing just doesn't make it. Anyone who has ever read a transcript of a meeting understands this without explanation. Transcribed speech is redundant, incomplete, circular, elliptical—a whole string of attributes that serve to puzzle and turn off the reader.

When the Hand Takes Over

Virtually everyone who has ever done any writing has experienced a time when the brain-hand pathway was completely open. The most easily remembered experience was in college, when you wrote frantically at the end of a three-hour exam to get all your thoughts down. Then, when you left the examination room, you couldn't even remember all the things you wrote. If you reread your exam later, you were surprised at the points you made; you had no memory of writing such things (good or bad). The reason your memory of the exam was so fuzzy was that you were using a brain-hand pathway that you don't recall as speech. It wasn't speech. It was writing.

The same thing happens regularly in any large-scale writing job. You reach a point where the beginning jitters have dis-appeared, and you get down to the business of writing. You may have to go back through all the pencil-sharpening, coffee-drinking routines every time you sit down again, but each time you work for a while, this fluency returns.

Our first aim in this chapter is to help you find a technique to open this brain-hand pathway quickly, easily, and dependably. We want you to find a way to avoid the coffee, the cigarettes, the desk cleaning, the pacing. We want you to sit down and write—no nonsense.

Setting Your Environment

As the first step, pay attention to the environment in which you write. Be sure you have enough light, that you're reasonably comfortable, that you have coffee if you need it, that you have plenty of paper and whatever else you need. The next step is make up your mind not to fiddle with that environment:

1. Don't spend time cracking knuckles, shuffling paper, sharpening pencils, or arranging pens in artistic patterns on the desk.
2. Don't pick up your equipment and play with it. That means don't chew on your pencils or pens, among other things. Holding your pencil in your hand waiting for inspiration is roughly comparable to walking around with your mouth open waiting to talk. You can easily become accustomed to playing with pencils and paper clips instead of using them for writing. If that happens, then you begin playing even when you properly pick them up—instead of writing.
3. Don't fool yourself into thinking that adding distractions to your writing environment will help you write. Turn off the radio.

Once you've set your environment, you're ready to write.

writing Versus Writing

The next thing you do is realize that there are two processes known as writing. One is a slightly mystical creative process that we might label *Writing*. Writing is done by Writers; they produce Books, Speeches, Fiction, Articles. Then there is plain old writing; this sort of writing is done by writers. They produce letters, memos, reports, recommendations.

Try not to confuse the two processes. You don't have to be a Writer to be a writer. And in the real world, the world that business and government operate in, the writers dominate. A large corporation's office tower may contain a few Writers, who produce Ads, PR, Annual Reports, and the like. On the other hand, virtually everyone who survives in business has to write something nearly every day—whether it be a memo to subordinates, a letter to a client, or a report on a new piece of equipment.

How can an auditor improve his position (or even do his job) if he can't write a decent audit report? How can a chemist show her worth if she can't properly document her experiments? How can a marketing expert help an organization if he can't get a letter out to a complaining client? It's true that secretaries help. So do innovations such as word processing centers, which clean up our writing messes for us. But important documents should not depend on the intuition of a secretary or a word-processing-machine operator for their effect.

It's a commonplace observation that the people who rise in business are well-spoken, highly political persons. It is also true that people who rise in business can usually deliver an effective written message. The key word there is *effective*. Don't mistake *effective* for *beautiful* or *elegant*. An effective message is one that transfers a message well. If your memos are never queried by those who receive them (and also aren't discarded), you may be an effective communicator already; you may have already mastered the mechanical process of writing. We'll be discussing the quality of writing in later chapters; what we're concentrating on now is getting that mechanical process going—fast and dependably.

Getting Your Pencil Moving

The most important part of sitting down to write is getting your hand going—forcing your brain to operate a writing apparatus at the expense of other things (distractions). So, when you sit down to write, the first thing you do is *write.* Now, that doesn't mean sit down like Shakespeare and dash off a brilliant memo. That means you sit down, pick up your pencil, and make your hand go. You open that pathway from your head to your hand—whatever way works best.

Business writing is a mechanical process (although there's some creativity to it—about the same amount as in carrying on a conversation). So you must approach it mechanically. Think for a moment about another mechanical activity: dancing. You go to a nightclub or a company function (the Christmas dance). The dance band begins to play. What is your first reaction? You tap your feet, or clap your hands, or hum—something to establish the rhythm in your body. Then you dance. When a new piece starts, you go through a miniversion of the same process again. You nod your head to the music a couple of times and begin. It's the same with writing. You have to get the process of head-hand communication going before you can expect anything to come out. What do you do? You start moving your pencil—and you keep it moving until your interest is concentrated on the paper.

What does that mean? It means something different for each person, obviously, because no two people operate precisely the same way. At some point, however, the room must seem to you to be centered on three things: your hand, a piece of paper, and a pencil (or pen or typewriter).

What to Do While Your Pencil Is Moving

Doodle. Draw cartoons. Copy out something famous from memory. "When in the course of human events, it becomes necessary. . . ." Do old-fashioned penmanship exercises, like push-pulls or circles. Write thirty words beginning with the letter q. Write thirty different names for the color red. Write the names of all the managers above you in the corporation. Write anything, draw anything—but keep your pencil moving and concentrate on what you're doing.

And be prepared for your speech apparatus to feel neglected; after all, it's used to doing your communicating. It's going to want something to eat, something to drink, something to smoke, someone to talk to. At the risk of sounding cute, you can't blame your mouth for wanting to take part in the activity. After all, you're accustomed to sending messages orally. And when you start conveying information on paper, you just naturally want to involve that familiar, easier instrument. So you chew on your pencil or your finger. You smoke. You drink coffee. Habit is a very potent enemy to writing, and your habits are linked primarily to listening and speaking, not to reading and writing. So you want the radio on, you want to talk it out with someone—instead of writing it out on paper.

Everyone has to deal with the problem in a different way. Maybe you chew gum; maybe you smoke; maybe you drink coffee; maybe you eat chocolates. Maybe you're able to ignore it. But don't be unaware of it—and realize what it is when it hits. Don't mistake your mouth's whining "me too" attitude for something that it isn't. Especially don't mistake it for a block to writing.[1] Writing is a bodily function as well as a cerebral one, and there's no point flying in the face of reality.

---

1. *Remember too that your mouth is closely connected to your intestinal tract. That's why you have to go to the bathroom immediately when you sit down to write.*

You have two jobs when you sit down to write:

1. Keep your pencil moving.
2. Cope with your mouth.

How to Get Something Down that Means Something

Sooner or later, of course, the doodles have to give way to something meaningful, or they, too, can become a distraction. But you don't have to jump right into a draft of what you're writing. You still don't have to cogitate on an opening sentence.

During our discussion of particles of meaning, we said that there's a body of information (storage-level particles) that represents the guts of your message. That's where to start. Once you have your hand moving painlessly, wander into the subject area a word at a time. Just write down some key words, some key concepts. Don't labor them, just jot them down and move on. Generally one thought will stir another—and since you're now communicating solely with yourself, you have no obligation to make sense, to stay within reality, to stay within the common boundaries of grammar.

Let's try an example. Say you're in product marketing for an office supply house, and you have to write a catalog description of a paper clip (it may sound unlikely, but go along for a moment). You put a paper clip in the middle of your desk, you stare at it, and you make your hand go. What happens? A few squiggly lines, and a few words. Your paper may look something like figure 3.1. The words you came up with may make no sense to anyone other than you, but they're a beginning—because there are some good observations about paper clips there: "metal, round, silver, about 4-5 inches long, twisted in shape, 3 bends." From those few words, you should be able to go on to a pretty decent description of a paper clip (try to write one; it's not easy). Rearrange those words a bit, add whatever is missing, and you've got it.

Figure 3.1. Paper clip notes.

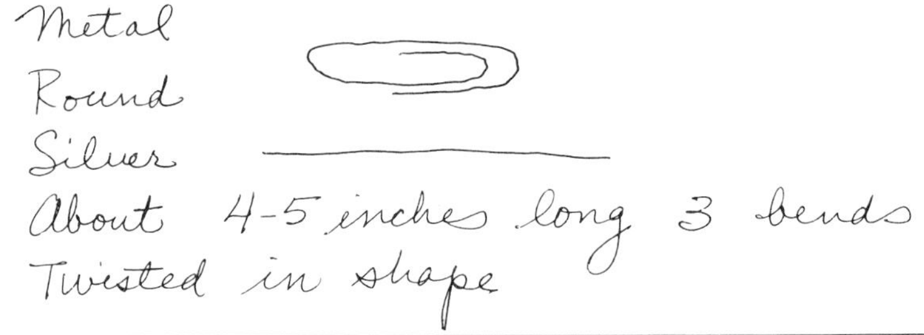

Automatic Writing

What you just did with the paper clip is a variant on a process that art historians and psychologists call automatic writing. The technique had a brief fling as an art form just after World War I, when the Dada group elevated nonsense to international artistic importance. Dada writers were fond of holding pencils to paper while they performed various tasks—to see what scratchings their minds would yield.

Be that as it may. Automatic writing is an extremely useful technique to the writing pragmatist. It's one of the easiest ways available of opening the pathway from the head to the hand.

From Head to Hand

When you're writing fluently, easily, smoothly, you're recording with your hand impulses that originate in your brain. Those impulses (ideas) are circuited directly to your writing, with no detours. When you're beginning to write or having difficulty writing, that direct flow of information from the brain to the hand is not well established. What most people tend to do when they write is translate verbal messages to paper. They formulate messages that they would speak if they could and then translate them into the symbols that constitute the written language. If you watch a room full of students taking a final examination, you'll see their lips move as they compose their first few sentences. They are talking to themselves; they're only writing as a sort of secretarial process.

Many of us are familiar with the same process in reading. We were all told as children not to mouth the words we read—but some continue to do so. It's a detouring of messages that severely limits the chance the reader has of getting the message straight. You may have heard that speed readers have better comprehension of what they read than do traditional, slower readers. It's true. Why? A speed reader bypasses completely the oral/aural impulse, and inputs his read information directly from his eyes to his brain. Likewise, the effective writer sends his ideas directly to his hand, totally bypassing the urge to talk. The flow of information to the hand produces *written language* in a much purer form than translations to paper of would-be spoken thoughts.

What are the differences between spoken and written language? The most obvious is that written language properly consists of complete sentences; spoken language is much looser in its construction. Written language is more formal, simply because it is more deliberate and is apt to have a longer life. Your words, when spoken, disappear as soon as the sound dies away. Your words, when written, may last longer than you expect (or want) in somebody's files. Consequently, you should feel the necessity of making your written messages worthy of a long life.

The ability to open the line of communication between your head and your hand is a learned skill (not a talent, not an art). It's like driving or dancing or skiing or typing. And, like those skills, it takes practice, combined with a decent technique. Automatic writing is a good device for such practice, and it's a good technique for getting started whenever you sit down to write.

What Does Automatic Writing Accomplish?

Ideally, automatic writing accomplishes the same thing that a woman accomplishes when she dumps out everything in her handbag to find a specific item. It helps you empty your mind of extraneous thoughts and pick out the ideas you want to pursue further. It also opens up a direct line of communication with your hand.

Consider the following situation. You're asked to write a quick summary of yesterday's meeting with the sales staff. The summary will be circulated in the department's weekly activity report. You don't know where to begin, so you write the phrase "Sales Meeting" at the top of a sheet of paper and stare at it while you do some automatic writing. Your paper might look like figure 3.2. Now there's a lot of information there and not all of it belongs

Figure 3.2. Automatic writing for activity report on sales meeting.

Bill - Jim - Susan - Me - Hoover
Hot room full of smoke
everybody in bad mood
Sales down returns high
on new line pressure on
for solution - decided to do
Customer survey on ads, maybe
questionnaire on returns - Jim
will follow up with legal

in the report. But notice that the things that came out first are the things you don't want to discuss. Items like "room full of smoke, everybody in bad mood" aren't the stuff that good reports are made of. But they interfere with your remembrance of the event, and so they cascade out of your brain with the other, more pertinent, information. Once they're out, you can consciously discard them and use the things you want to use. In addition, since the thoughts came out first in the shape of written words, you've got a decent chance of opening up the path from your head to your hand with relative ease.

If you use automatic writing consistently for a period of time (a month, a week—it varies), you'll find that it works.

Other Things that Go Bump While You Write

Many writing assignments contain unsolvable problems that get in your way while you're trying to communicate. It's hard to say what to do with them. Examples might include:

1. You don't know the person you're writing to, so you don't know how well-versed he or she is in the subject.
2. You know your performance is being monitored with particular care on this project, for one reason or another—and you feel like someone is looking over your shoulder all the time.
3. You are rushed and/or unfamiliar with the subject matter.

Practice Makes Perfect

Just like your old basketball coach used to tell you, you've got to practice a skill to improve it—or even to maintain it. If you're a good ice skater who hasn't skated for a few years, you're going to be wobbly on the ice. If you're a good writer who doesn't find it necessary to write often, you're not going to be a good writer for long. If you're not a good writer, and don't write often, you're going to backslide, too. If you are serious about wanting to make it easier to sit down and write, you must do it regularly and frequently, so you'll develop the necessary mental skills—the switching mechanisms that allow you to turn off your mouth and turn on your hand.

One of the techniques we recommend is keeping a business journal for a time. Determine for yourself in advance how long you'll keep it; we suggest ninety days. Then get a desk calendar that gives you a place to write under each date.[2] The rest is simple;

---

2. *Two nationally known products of this type are the "Weekly Planner" and the "Week at a Glance" journals. Your stationer is probably familiar with both if you aren't.*

you commit to yourself to write one hundred words each and every weekday summarizing the day's business. Try to write intelligibly, but don't concern yourself with grammar; this journal is addressed to you. You'll find that, at the end of the ninety-day period, your ability to sit down and write will be much improved. What will you have learned? You'll have taught your body to communicate on command in writing.

Not only is such a journal a good practice tool in writing, it's an excellent business procedure. Your ability to recall data will amaze people; your familiarity with your own calendar will make you more efficient. It doesn't take much time to write one hundred words; it's just ten lines of ten words each. And it's amazing what the exercise can do for fluency and "writing nerves."

Once you can sit down to write with something approaching ease, you can begin working on knocking 'em dead with your organization, clarity, elegance, brevity, and precision. If you need work in any of those areas, read on.

Exercises

1. Write down on a piece of paper the name of the projects you have been working on. Now apply the method of automatic writing. Select one project from the list and write down items of progress. Progress and activity reports are difficult to write since they must be short, convey events, and provide continuity.
2. Examine your writing environment—desk, chair, pens, pencils, etc. Try out different arrangements of furniture as well as use of different writing instruments. These changes may create a better atmosphere in which to write.

For each of the subjects in exercises 3 through 7, write down sentence-level and storage-level particles. Use automatic writing.

3. Personnel evaluation of someone in your department.
4. The efficiency and cost of operating your car.
5. A request for several tax forms.
6. A letter to a department store regarding a billing error.
7. A sales pitch for a brand of soap to be printed on the side of the bar wrapper.

8. In your next staff or department meeting, write down particles as the meeting progresses. File the list away until the minutes of the meeting are distributed. Compare the list and the minutes. Did the minutes convey all of the particles?

9. Follow through on the ninety-day journal idea we proposed in this chapter. Develop a method to evaluate your progress in writing the journal.

4

Logic and Arguments: How to Convince Your Audience

very time you write or talk, you're doing two things: sending a message and exposing yourself. Imagine, for example, that you've recently been promoted to a new job, and your first assignment is to evaluate the department's need for a new generation of computing equipment. The recommendation you'll make is no secret; you've already discussed it with your new boss—and he has concurred with your analysis. But, to get authorization for a large expenditure, a written recommendation is in order. That report will be forwarded up the line of management over your boss's signature. Because your manager will be signing the report, he will be inclined to be critical of your style. You feel especially exposed.

We've used this situation to point out something that goes on all the time. People judge you by the quality of your communication. In business, first impressions count for much. And, in business, first impressions (and subsequent ones as well) are made largely on the basis of either letters or conversations. The whole tone of a relationship can be set by your willingness to perfect your communicating style. Consider, too: as a white-collar worker, your only visible products are probably written documents. It doesn't make good sense on any plane to put out a second-rate effort on something so obviously important to your future. A change of management or a simple review of the files can throw unexpected importance on your writing, your thought processes, and your logic.

The most important documents you will generate in your business life are those that set out to persuade somebody to do something. Consequently, those documents are the ones for which you must concentrate most heavily on your image in communicating. Does each letter, each memo, each report you write say to its audience that you are well-informed, articulate, well-spoken, sensible, and eminently promotable?

This chapter on logic and arguments will deal with the documents you most need to perfect—persuasive ones. Remember, we're still in the process of structuring thoughts in terms of the communications path, but we're beginning to move toward putting definite language on those structures. Persuasive communications (or *arguments,* as they are properly termed) are the first line of attack.

Types of Arguments

Most of the things you write or speak are meant to be read or heard by someone.[1] In a very real sense, everything you write or speak has an element of persuasion in it ("read me"). Even utterances that are strictly informational have different weights coming from different people. The most obvious difference derives from standing in society. For example:

> If Mr. Smith down the street says the community's schools ought to be more completely integrated, it merits some attention—particularly if Mr. Smith is articulate, well-informed, and well-spoken. People will listen. But if the Supreme Court says that the community's schools ought to be more completely integrated, that's a different matter. People don't stand around and ponder whether or not to comply; they have no choice.

That's a good illustration of different weights from different standings in society. Everybody knows, for instance, that the higher on the company organization chart you are, the more attention your opinion commands.

But accepting the fact that each of us has a current standing in society (no matter how much we intend to improve ourselves in

---

1. *Or else you oughtn't to write them.*

the future), most of us have to live with less influence than the Supreme Court has. Consequently, when we want something done, we must expend more effort getting it done. That means that if you want people to pay attention when you write—you have to convince them that it's worth their while to do so. That's the most important argument you face—and it's perpetual. You must convince, reconvince, and re-reconvince them. If you look like a fool once, you ruin everything.

In addition to the diurnal "you ought to listen to me" argument, there are other easily identifiable types:

1. You ought to accept Proposal A (instead of B or C) for the reasons . . .
2. We need an increase over last year's budget because . . .
3. Vote for Candidate Zabriskie because . . .
4. Buy Sudso Detergent.
5. We need another secretary in our group because . . .
6. We should decline the merger even though it looks good, because . . .

Keeping in mind that people won't listen to you unless you win the first argument, let's examine the ways in which you can approach these.

Argumentative Stances

What is an argument anyway? The word has several meanings, but we're dealing with just one: "an address or composition intended to convince or persuade."[2] Let's look at an example before we begin to categorize things. Randall Stewart, general manager of the firm of Elco Electronics, has asked three of his employees to respond to the following memorandum:

To: James Blake, Linda Thompson, Wendell Philips
From: Randall Stewart
Subject: Recommendation on Semiconductors

As you know, we have been considering the proposal to stop manufacturing semiconductors and to concentrate instead on supplying components to two computer manufacturers. Please give me your recommendations by Friday. Thanks.

---

2. The Random House College Dictionary, rev. ed. (New York: Random House, 1975).

The first to respond is Ms. Thompson, who is a member of the company's accounting staff:

To: Randall Stewart
From: Linda Thompson
Subject: Recommendation on Semiconductors

This note is in response to yours on the continued manufacture of semiconductors. The economic arguments are quite clear: there is still a good profit in our existing semiconductor line. Even with a 40 percent decline (unlikely in even the most pessimistic market estimates), the line would be profitable. The semiconductor line currently contributes 23 percent of total sales and 28 percent of total profit.

It's a good memo; it has a valid point to make. It's straightforward and brief, clear and concise.

The second memo is from Mr. Blake:

To: Randall Stewart
From: James Blake
Subject: Recommendation on Semiconductors

I don't see how the question of discontinuing semiconductors ever came up in the first place. Semiconductors are what built Elco up, and what has kept us here for the past ten years. And right now, we're selling almost as many as we can turn out. Morale would nose-dive if we made such a decision—and what kind of impact would it make on our investors if we told them that? Think what the semiconductor business (and our valuable clients) have done for us, and I'm sure you'll agree with me.

Another well-written, brief, to-the-point memo. No arguments about style, about the flow of thought, about the intentions of the writer. Mr. Blake has taken a forceful position, and has several important points in his favor—especially the point he makes about the impact on investors and shareholders.

The third respondent, Wendell Philips, takes yet another tack:

To: Randall Stewart
From: Wendell Philips
Subject: Discontinuing Semiconductors

I recommend that we take steps to cease production of semi-conductors as soon as feasible.

My impressions of the future of the semiconductor business are quite discouraging to the current operation. Those impressions are based on a gut reaction on my part, and on my contacts with various other veterans in the field. Things are beginning to sag, and there's no tightening of the trend in sight.

It seems certain to me that all major semiconductor manufacturers will begin conversion to other systems within the short range—maybe we should lead the pack, get dug in with a replacement technology, and grab a part of whatever the new market will be before the rest of the industry wolves get there. I'll be happy to discuss my recommendations for conversion at your convenience.

Now, the three respondents each had a specific approach to the subject of semiconductors and the semiconductor business. They are representative of the three major types of argument, or persuasion, that are available to most communicators. They are:

1. logical argument
2. emotional argument
3. argument by personal image

We'll examine these types of argument one by one, but first let us emphasize that all three types of argument are fair techniques. None of them violates ethics or argues from false premises. All three have a valid place in business—and the well-rounded communicator is a master of them all.

Logical Arguments

We were brought up as good Americans to believe that the logical approach to anything is the best approach. Indeed, since the *philosophes* of the eighteenth century initiated the Age of Reason, the whole Western world has spent its largest and most spectacular efforts in pursuit of logic: scientific, mathematical, economical, financial, mechanical. Computers are monuments to logic, to the reduction of logic to millions of tiny yes/no mechanical operations. And, lest we sound antilogic, let us hasten to add that logic is indeed a powerful instrument in the hands of a capable communicator. It has the force of 250 years' faith behind it, together with the "let's-be-logical-about-this" schooling we've all had. It has some problems, too:

1. Logic is seldom perfect, and so is open to defeat.
2. The evidence used to support logic is frequently open to

varying interpretations—and so to varying lines of logic.
3. There is no room in a logical sequence for any kind of opinion, feeling, imponderable—nothing, in short, that is not quantifiable.
4. Logic invites rebuttal.[3]

Obviously, there are times when logic is the only answer. Those times are characteristically investigative situations. For example, say you want to buy a new car, and the only model on the market that really turns you on is the Mercedes 450SEL, which costs a cool $22,000 or more. A logical sequence proper to many situations like this is:

1. I want a Mercedes 450SEL, but
2. I cannot afford a Mercedes 450SEL; therefore, regretfully
3. I will not buy a Mercedes 450SEL. (Sigh).

A result from a more complex version of the same logic might be a governmental decision to defer plans to build a new dam until sufficient funding is allocated by Congress. Obviously the evidence in such a syllogism would be more complex, but the line of logic would (or should) be the same. But frequently we try to rely on logic when it isn't the most forceful (or even the most appropriate) weapon in our argumentative armory. And, more dangerous, illogical arguments are sometimes presented as though they were logical. Consider, for example, the following version of the 450SEL syllogism presented above:

1. I want a Mercedes 450SEL, but
2. I cannot afford a Mercedes 450SEL; but
3. I love it so much I'm going to buy it anyway.

The three lines are presented in the format of a logical argument, but the illogic of the conclusion might be painfully obvious to a lending institution approached to finance the vehicle. It might not be as obvious to the car buyer. He might be inclined to say something like, "I thought it out, and it's expensive, but I can make the payments." The phrase, "I thought it out," implies a logical decision was made—and the car buyer may actually believe that the decision he made was logical. But it wasn't; it was emotional.

---

3. *Aristotle used faultless logic to prove that a heavy rock will fall faster than a light rock. But it isn't true: they fall at the same rate, as Galileo found out 2,000 years after Aristotle. So much for the usefulness of faultless logic!*

On a complex interpersonal level, pseudological arguments are more common than truly logical ones. Look back, for instance, at Linda Thompson's memo to Randall Stewart on the subject of semiconductors (page 55). Note the third sentence:

"Even with a 40 percent decline (unlikely in even the most pessimistic market estimates), the line would be profitable."

Sounds like a logical statement, well-researched, presented in a nondeceptive, straightforward manner. But it isn't all those things, because it cannot be an accurate statement as it stands. There's no indication of a time period anywhere in the sentence. Certainly a 40 percent drop-off in sales beginning suddenly tomorrow won't have the same effect that a gradual drop-off (perhaps accompanied by progressive layoffs, plant closings, other retrenchments) will have. And certainly a line that experiences a gradual 40 percent drop-off is a moribund line, one with no future but further and further falling sales. The clue is that market estimates are always contained in a time frame ("We expect sales declines of 20 percent to 27 percent *over the next six months*"), and Linda Thompson has falsely extrapolated a figure without its accompanying (and qualifying) milieu. So what Linda Thompson is doing—probably with little awareness on her part—is presenting a biased case, based on a one-sided interpretation of facts. It isn't a logical argument as presented, although it certainly appears to be. A perceptive Randall Stewart would have to reject it as not well thought out.

Logic can be a powerful tool when it's applicable, irrefutable, and accurate. But there's nothing that can destroy your credibility as completely as a hole in your logic. An audience will never forget catching you in a logical faux pas, and readers won't trust you as long as they remember you tried to put one over on them. Logic is best saved for times when it is unarguably appropriate, when imponderables are at a minimum, and when the facts and their interpretation are in general agreement. Even when it's used absolutely properly, however, logic isn't necessarily the most effective possible style of argument; it remains cold, inflexible, and challenging to rebuttal.

Emotional Arguments

Just as we were brought up to respect logic, or the appearance of logic, we were trained to avoid emotion ("Let's keep our personal feelings out of this"). Emotion is viewed as unbusinesslike and dangerous when it's termed "emotion." Disguised as other things, it's more often accepted. No one dismisses "gut reaction" or "sixth sense" or "tradition" or "sneaky hunches" the way they do emotion. But, of course, all those things are just particular aspects of emotion in business—legitimate uses of emotion.

The memo on semiconductors submitted by James Blake is strong on emotional arguments—both legitimate and not so legitimate. It's a good illustration of the strengths and weaknesses of the emotional approach to business. What are Blake's strengths? First of all, his wide-ranging concern for the people involved. He is the only one of the three respondents who worries about personnel and shareholder morale—an extremely important consideration, and one that is best considered from an emotional point of view (morale is an extended form of emotion). Blake's reaction may very well be a good indicator of what Elco will face if they decide to discontinue semiconductors. A wise Elco management would prepare for the onslaught of morale problems with a well-planned internal and external public relations campaign.

What, on the other hand, are Blake's outstanding weaknesses? In a few words, a total lack of entrepreneurial spirit, combined with an overriding dependence on the past. You will find, surprisingly, that emotion tends to dominate in two types of business arguments:

1.   arguments to maintain the status quo
2.   arguments to apply a standing principle, whether that principle is a matter of ethics or simple procedure[4]

It appears to be easier for most people to construct emotional arguments on these two topics than to construct logical ones. It also appears to be quite difficult to construct any emotional arguments other than these two; it seems nearly impossible to construct an emotional argument for innovation, for example. Emotional arguments are most often used and most often effective when they're on the side of tradition. Emotional arguments are frequently used to "do things like we always have," or to "avoid

---

4.   *Which doesn't preclude emotion from running both sides of an argument. Consider the ongoing battle over the issue of abortions in the United States, for example. Both sides are battling for established principles: proabortion groups argue for individual liberties (certainly sacred in the United States); right-to-life groups argue for motherhood and against so-called murder.*

change for change's sake," or to "make an example of this case," or to "treat everyone the same to avoid making waves."[5]

James Blake seems unwilling to look into the future without the props and mainstays of the past as comforts—almost as security blankets. He lugs around the semiconductor business as part of his well-being, very much the way a child hauls around a teddy bear. But he belies the value of his argument in his own words: "And right now, we're selling almost as many as we can turn out." Obviously, production capability now surpasses demand. While that may be a temporary setback due to market slack or time of year, there's no indication of such a predictable loss in Blake's communication. Indicators are, given Blake's overall attitude, that he is refusing to face up to market trends.

Just as there are pitfalls in logical arguments, there are predictable traps in emotional arguments:

1. They are inclined to be backward-looking, rather than forward—to argue for maintenance of the status quo at the expense of all change.
2. Emotion frequently defies logic. Although it may thereby point out the deficiencies in logic, it frequently falls short of a sensible mark itself.
3. Emotional arguments frequently limit breadth of vision. Just as Blake limited his view of the supply/demand picture in semiconductors, the emotional arguer frequently blinkers out whole segments of the world in his attempt to justify the status quo.

Emotional arguments often masquerade as logical arguments, to further complicate the picture. Recall the "logic" that justified purchase of the Mercedes 450SEL. These arguments from hidden emotion can be identified because they are defined by one or more of the descriptions we listed. Always examine extra carefully any logical progression that argues blindly for the status quo or that uses buzzwords; it may turn out to be a strictly emotional statement in its underpinnings.

Few arguments are strictly logical or strictly emotional, but it's useful to sort out the components when structuring your own arguments. It's also indispensable to be able to distinguish between the two modes when receiving a message (see chapter 10, "Reading for Meaning").

---

5. This holds true in politics as well. Liberals are intellectuals whose primary facade is logic. Conservatives are often emotional traditionalists who see themselves as the bastions of principle and historical spirit. Liberals see conservatives as irrational; conservatives see liberals as eggheads. There are, of course, exceptions—but surprisingly few.

Arguments by Personal Image

A third mode of argument rests on personal image. To illustrate the mode, let us retell an unconfirmed story about a great twentieth-century British thinker. It seems that this scholar handed the manuscript for one of his many books to his publisher totally devoid of footnotes. He simply gave no references for anything he said. An earnest young copy editor questioned the great man on his reasons for making some rather sweeping unsubstantiated statements. The author replied, "Young man, there is no point to being an expert if you have to bolster your thoughts with those of other people."

Whether or not the story is true (and it sounds too good to be), it makes a point about this third mode of argument. If you can argue from a position of personal prominence, of unquestioned information, so much the better. It is unquestionably the most potent of the three modes of argument—and equally unquestionably the most difficult one to use. Nevertheless, because of its potency, it's worth cultivating.

For illustration's sake, let's look at the components of personal image arguments as though they were neatly divisible into two categories: wisdom and articulation. The wisdom category might be represented by an inarticulate but brilliant scientist (for obvious reasons, we'll use no names). His word is legal tender in his profession—but the only way to get that word is to pry it out of him and translate it into understandable English. He's without articulation almost completely; nevertheless, substantial respect is accorded his knowledge and experience. Articulation might be represented by a politician (or businessman, teacher, writer) who is gifted with a glib tongue and a polished, authoritative style. Because of his impeccable command of the language and his forcefulness, he too becomes an authority. The best-seller lists are good hunting grounds for these types, as are newspaper columns and television commentaries.

If you are in a position to invoke either of these types of personal image, you're fortunate indeed. The unfortunate fact is that few of us are so privileged. Nevertheless, there are ways in which we can make use of the technique. Let's begin with Wendell Philips's memo on semiconductors. We have no indication that Mr. Philips is any more or less an authority than either of the other two respondents. But there's a difference in tone, in confidence, and in thrust in his memo evident at even a first reading. Philips is bold, direct, brief, and open; he makes his position of authority known ("a gut reaction on my part, and . . .

my contacts with various other veterans in the field"). Obviously, anyone in Philips's position is a man worth listening to. Why?

It's a matter of stance and viewpoint. Notice, first of all, that Philips uses himself as a point of reference consistently. His first sentence begins, "I recommend . . ." and the tone remains self-confident throughout. He identifies himself with the company quite readily ("maybe *we* should lead the pack, get dug in with a replacement technology, and grab a part of . . . the new market"). Philips's language is firm, pointed, and strong. Look at the strength of his choice of words: "lead the pack," "grab the new market." Those are the words of a man who knows what he's talking about.

It's difficult to escape the notion that Philips is the most capable of the three respondents. He has argued from a position of prominence—even though there's no indication that he's more important to Elco than the other two. His logic is entrepreneurial, forward-looking; his grasp of the situation seems to be well-balanced and well-rounded. He has no fear of emotion; indeed, he trusts his intuition ("gut reaction"). But he touches all bases, and he responds more directly to the original request for recommendations than either Blake or Thompson.

What's to be learned from Philips's memo? Simply that a firm, clear, self-confident approach to communication makes a far better impression than either impeccable logic or powerful emotion. It's a lesson that can profitably be transferred to daily communication.

The simple fact is that you're judged as much on your presentation as you are on your material. Seasoned businessmen are already aware of that sometimes painful reality. And you must take it upon yourself to make your presentations as powerful, as confident, as thorough, as elegant, and as brief as they can possibly be—to best serve your own interests. When that effort is expended, an extra dividend is provided as well: you transcend logic and emotion, and speak from the rarefied air of personal image. If your reader perceives you as unsure or awkward or grammatically incorrect, you lose points in his estimation. If your reader sees you as intelligent and self-confident, you've got a jump on the game. What we've said is easily summed up:

1.   Use logic and emotion carefully and knowledgeably, and be aware of their flaws.
2.   Don't depend entirely on either logic or emotion; they each provide valuable tests for the validity of the other.

3. When you can add personal image to your arsenal of persuasion, you have an added chance of succeeding.

How Is Personal Image Created?

You're building a personal image of some kind every time you communicate. Whether that image is positive or negative or noncommittal depends on the quality of your communication. Generally, literate, confident messages engender a positive personal image response.

How do you write messages geared to create a positive personal image? Chapter 5 (coming up) was written to give you some guidelines in just that. But before we move on to techniques of writing, savor the peak of personal image in the form of the following editorial, entitled "No," written by former Senator Sam J. Ervin, Jr. Senator Sam has always claimed to be "just a simple country lawyer," but his writing tells a different story. It is a near-perfect synthesis of fine logic tempered by lightly emotional language—all delivered from a position of prominence unmatched by many other writers.

No

By Sam J. Ervin Jr.

I fear that my former colleagues in the United States Congress, eager to rid politics of the last remnants of Watergate-type scandals, may be close to damaging the very institution they hope to strengthen.

Several proposals have been introduced in both the House of Representatives and the Senate that would provide for taxpayer financing of Congressional campaigns in much the same manner as the Presidential campaigns are financed.

What they may fail to recognize, however, in their zeal to remove any taint of special-interest money, is not only the potentially terrible financial burden they may be laying on the taxpayers' shoulders but the damage they may be doing to the election system itself.

Under many of the proposals being considered, only minimal requirements are established before Federal funds are made available to Congressional candidates. One proposal in the House even extends the concept beyond the general election to include primaries as well. Thus, one net effect of the bills, if they become

---

law, would be the proliferation of splinter candidates or one-issue candidates, much as we saw in the early days of the Presidential campaign last year.

This proliferation of campaigns and individual candidacies would have two detrimental effects on the electoral system. First, it would tend to drain the Federal funds early in the primary season, with a large number of candidates drawing from the Federal till. And, second, it would tend to accelerate the demise of the two-party system on the national level, leading us down the coalition road already traveled by many Western allies.

One of the most compelling arguments against taxpayer financing of Congressional campaigns is that, according to the Internal Revenue Service, only about 25 percent of the United States taxpayers have gone along with the dollar checkoff for Presidential elections on their income tax returns. Thus, if the process is expanded to include Congressional campaigns without a parallel expansion of public interest and participation, the United States Treasury might be forced to underwrite political campaigns out of tax monies pledged for other, more worthwhile projects.

Administratively the proposals would cause outrageous havoc. In testimony before the House Administration Committee recently, Ralph K. Winter, professor of law at Yale University said: "It has been estimated that the auditing of 15 Presidential candidates consumed 35 person-years of labor by the Federal Election Commission in 1976." He rightly concludes that a proposed expansion from those 15 Presidential candidates to possibly more than 1,000 Congressional candidates refutes itself.

Further, public funding would place in one executive-branch agency, the Federal Election Commission, large-scale discretion-ary enforcement power that could increase the potential for election-year mischief, similar to what we saw exposed a few years ago.

Delays in processing the required forms could leave candi-dates without any funds during critical periods in the campaign and it would be virtually impossible to determine later whether those delays were bureaucratic or political.

My former colleagues should consider measures looking to taxpayer financing of Congressional campaigns by amendments to the income tax laws giving taxpayers increased tax credits or deductions for political contributions to Congressional candi-dates. This would tend to stimulate more open political debate in Congressional campaigns, for it would require Congressional candidates to appeal directly to taxpayers for financial assistance.

And after that eloquence, we rest our case.

Exercises

Analyze each of the memos in exercises 1 through 3 and determine which type of argument is being used. Discuss the effectiveness of the memo.

1. To: Roger Warner
    From: Sandra Banning
    Subject: New 8090 Typewriter

    I have now had the opportunity to observe the new 8090 typewriter compared to our currently used model-7110. A test was conducted with three secretaries over a one-week period. The 8090 was found to be quieter, faster (a 20 percent increase in speed), and more compact.

2. To: Margaret Tracy
    From: James Landsford
    Subject: Office Furniture

    This note is to summarize my review of the APCOM line of office furniture in use at our REVCO division. It appears to be very comfortable and functional. Employees used the furniture, however, the prices are somewhat higher than our current brand. Also, it would take time for our staff to adjust to the new furniture. It is recommended that we stay with our current furniture.

3. To: Ramsey Losche
    From: Paul Winer
    Subject: Review of Request for New Office Space by Accounting

    I have reviewed the request by accounting for an additional 10,000 square feet of office space. Accounting currently suffers from a severe space shortage. Providing this space will increase efficiency to the same degree as my previous study of purchasing. It is one of the most justified requests that I have received.

4. For each memo in exercises 1 through 3, formulate a new memo using a different type of argument.

In each of the following situations, you are to write a letter. Discuss how each type of argument could be used in writing the letter. Having selected an argument type, compose a letter.

5. You are a patient of Dr. Jones and have been billed twice for the same services.
6. You never got your refund check from the federal government. It is three months overdue.
7. Last year you made a loan of $500 to Uncle Harry who lives 2,000 miles away. He has not paid anything on the loan for a year.
8. You are a plant manager at a steel mill. Your factory will shut down unless EPA emission standards are waived for one year. (You are to write the EPA.)
9. Look at three memos and/or letters you have received in response to your notes. Also find a copy of your original letter in each case. Do the following:
   a. Classify each of your letters as to type of argument.
   b. Classify each response as to type of argument.
   c. Evaluate the result of the response. If it was negative, analyze your type of argument. Could your letter have had a better chance with a different type? If it was positive, why did it occur?
10. The review of the Sam Ervin editorial is a good example of what you need to do—analyze other people's writing and see its flaws and strengths. Go through a newspaper to the editorial page. Evaluate the writing and appropriateness of two newspaper editorials—one written by a so-called expert and another by an interested citizen. Do this on a regular basis. You'll be able to improve your own writing.

5

Decisions, Decisions

The law punishes premeditated crime more rigorously than it does unpremeditated crime. Why? Because premeditation involves intent, resolve, and, above all, planning. In communication, premeditation is the single qualifier that distinguishes a consistently good writer from the pack. Premeditated writing gives you control over what you write, how you write it, and to whom you write it. It enables you to say exactly what you want to say, nothing more and nothing less—which, as you may recall, is pretty close to the definition of successful communication.

This chapter concentrates on premeditation: decisions that must be made prior to every important written communication. Once you answer all the questions, make all the decisions discussed in this chapter, you'll be as well-informed a writer as anyone could ask. You'll know everything you can find out about:

> your message
> your reader
> your medium

In addition, you'll know—in fairly precise terms—what the outcome of your communication should be regarding:

> feedback or action
> your personal image
> your relationship to the reader

Sounds like we're promising the moon, doesn't it? Maybe we are. But we believe all the important way stations are here. And anyway, you have to do all the hard work yourself. We aren't giving away prepackaged decisions here—no, indeed.

Communications as War

Imagine for a moment that you are a member of the Joint Chiefs of Staff in Washington, D.C. You are chairing a meeting in the War Room. The year is 1943, and the tide in World War II is just beginning to turn in favor of the Allies. This meeting will discuss three important topics:

1. objective
2. strategy
3. tactics

These three concepts are all-important to our conduct of the war effort. They might be defined in the context of the war as:

1. Objective: Win the war by retaking the fallen countries and invading Germany.
2. Strategy: Encircle Berlin with an Allied pincer movement.
3. Tactics: All the details involved in implementing the encirclement strategy.

Now, return to the present, but bring with you an understanding of the three terms used in the War Room. This chapter will explore those three terms in the context of communicating messages. Getting a message across bears similarities to waging a war: any degree of failure can be disastrous, and only the most carefully plotted strategy can be totally successful.

Objective

We'll be laying out a string of decisions to be made during the course of this chapter. It's essential that they be made consciously and in order, prior to any important communication. Some of them will be almost automatic (as you'll see); others you may be inclined to skip over entirely in the rush of daily business. Skipping over any one of them can cause a partial failure in your message. Remember that your sole objective in communicating is to transfer a message from your head to the head of a receiver *intact*.

That objective puts you squarely in front of the first two decisions to be made before writing:

1. What storage-level particles of meaning do you mean to state?

2. What storage-level particles of meaning do you mean to imply?

Answering these two questions may be the most difficult part of getting ready to write—but, without concrete answers, you might as well not bother to go further. If you cannot phrase to yourself what you want your reader to know after you finish communicating, then put down your pen and wait. We're not suggesting that you produce an outline—not yet. Just make a list (on paper, so you won't forget anything) of the things you want to say, in any order. Remember that at this point you're communicating only with yourself, so you needn't worry about style, elegance, form, or any of the other components of a finished message. All you need is enough to indicate the whole message to you. It doesn't matter if the slip of paper would look like nonsense to the rest of the world—as long as you know what it means. That messy slip of paper will guide you through the whole "strategy" segment of our decision guide. It will act as a statement of your objectives in communicating; it is comparable to the War Room objective of "win the war."

Remember that there are some storage-level particles that you'll convey simply by the fact of your writing. You must be aware of them and include them automatically on your list of implied particles—unless you choose to make them explicit. They're various and important, and they include:

1. The impact of your relationship to the reader. You may be his boss, or he yours. You may be an important client, or he may not even know your name. You may be married to his sister. Each of these relationships adds an important implied particle to the message.
2. The impact of the origin of your message. Consider the difference between an unsolicited message, and one that is written in response to a stimulus generated by the reader ("Please send me some information on your product line" or "If I don't hear from you to the contrary I will assume . . .").

Be certain that your list of objectives is complete before you proceed to the strategy phase of message planning. It should contain every storage-level particle you expect to convey, including all the implied particles. To handle implication correctly and effectively, you must be constantly aware of what you're doing. If you find that people read into your memos things you didn't intend, you're not aware of the implied particles you're sending.

Strategy

With your objectives firmly in hand, you're ready to set some strategy—to decide how most effectively to get your message across. In the strategy phase, there are seven important decisions to be made and one task to be performed.

As with the objectives, we frequently skim over the decisions in the strategy planning phase. It's like breathing—you can't go around thinking about every breath you take. You'd go mad, or at best you'd become vegetative. There are simply some things that don't bear close analysis. Right? Wrong. With some practice, many of the strategy decisions can be made quickly—some of them automatically. But not mindlessly. Don't assume that any of the questions we pose are silly or trivial. If they were, we wouldn't be asking them. As any good cook knows, you add salt to certain dishes without thinking twice about it, but you don't dump in handfuls of it. The same goes for strategy in message planning—it needn't be labored, but it must be thoughtful. With that proviso, let's plunge ahead into the seven strategy decisions.

1. Format

Your first decision concerns the format of the message you've decided to send. It's based on the quantity and the importance of the storage-level particles you've compiled. Your choice of format is all-important to the conveyance of your message, and the format itself may be used to convey important implied particles. How? Let's look at a couple of examples.

Example A
You've decided to contact an associate in a different department on a matter that involves an EDP facility that you share. Because of time conflicts, you've decided to propose that your department use the computer on Tuesdays and Thursdays, leaving Mondays and Wednesdays for your associate's department. Fridays will still be up for grabs on an as-needed basis. What are your format choices?
1. A telephone call.
2. A personal visit.
3. An interoffice memorandum.
4. An interoffice memorandum with carbons to others.
5. A note on your "from the desk of" pad.

The differences between the formats are probably immediately obvious. Either of the two nonwritten messages will present a feeling of willingness to negotiate, of seeking mutual interest. The three written formats indicate various degrees of flexibility; the carbons to others (his boss, your boss, the data center) indicate that you've taken much of the responsibility for this decision on yourself—and have relegated your colleague to a reactive position. Personal and business relationships differ with the personalities involved—any of these formats may be acceptable, but they all impact the transfer of meaning in different ways. Your simple note may seem more friendly; it may also seem less important. Your memo with carbons may seem like a public goad; it may also seem like you're simply trying to pave the way to an agreement. Your judgment is the deciding factor.

Example B
You're responding to a request from a potential sales client for information on a specific product line. Your options include:

1. A brochure with price list.
2. A letter with a brochure and price list.
3. A letter suggesting that you'd like to call on the client.
4. A telephone call.

Any of these options may be appropriate, but a decision should be made—a conscious decision—about which one should be used. What factors should figure in your decision? The amount of business that might be generated, the quality of your brochure, your available time—that kind of thing.

2. Length—General
Your format decision will affect your decision on the general length of your message. If you've decided to write a memo, it will probably be short—one or two paragraphs. But if your format is less specific (such as a report, a position paper, or a letter), you must make a general decision about length. If you've been asked to compile a report on your department's business, you must decide early how long that report should be. What information should you use in making that decision? There are various considerations, including the amount of time you have, the amount of time your reader will have, the magnitude of the subject, and your ability (and/or willingness) to write.

It's a serious mistake to believe that the subject matter will dictate length during writing. Such a belief cripples your ability to balance your message and may account for some serious setbacks in your ability to transfer meaning. Most commonly, the idea that "it'll be as long as it needs to be" leads a writer to unnecessary verbosity at the beginning of a piece and unwarranted brevity at the end. You start off treating the subject very fully. Then you begin to tire of writing, and by the time the last section comes up, you're skipping important detail, abbreviating logic, omitting the very tactics that are most needed at the close of a document.

If you allocate space at the very beginning of the process ("This report should end up about twenty pages long"), you can plan the space you'll need for each and every important point—and you can pace yourself to give your best effort when it's most needed.

3. Method/Organization

Your next decision involves the method by which you'll unify your message. Basically, you decide your plan of attack—in broad terms. There are as many methods of organizing messages as there are messages themselves, but a couple of examples may help you understand the kind of thinking that must go on in this step.

Example A
You've been asked to write an evaluation of a pilot program that has just completed its first year of funding. You notice that the program is quite similar to another one undertaken several years earlier, and you decide to organize your report around a comparison of the two projects.

Example B
You're contacting a potential client who may be in the market for the product you represent. There's lots of competition for the contract, and you have to decide on a method of presentation that will single you out from the herd. You decide to organize your proposal around a hard-hitting analysis of your client's needs—and totally ignore the competition.

In each of these examples, you've chosen a method of presentation that will have a substantial impact on the shape the message will finally take. Most messages pass through this decision, even if it isn't apparent. For instance, if you're writing a personnel directive concerning tardiness, you must decide whether you'll begin by talking about the rash of tardiness that has prompted the message or by talking about company policy that is simply being restated from the employee manual.

4. Logic

Closely allied to the method/organization decision is a consideration of logic—and by the term we mean the broad flow of logic, not small details of it. Will you, for instance, argue largely from examples? From your position of authority? From data? From precedent? Will you state your conclusions plainly or leave the reader to draw what conclusions he will? Will you explain them chronologically or categorically? A couple of examples:

Example A
You're writing about various profit centers in your widely diversified corporation. You can choose a logic that talks first about 1974, then 1975, then 1976, then 1977, then 1978 (and so on). Alternatively you can choose a logic that says, in effect, "Let's consider each product line separately, analyzing trends and return on investment."

Example B
You're writing a press release that states your company's position on a piece of legislation pending in the state capitol. You might choose to start with previous attempts to pass such legislation; you might decide to talk about adverse effects on the state's economy. You might want to write merely about the additional incursion this legislation makes into the domain of private business. Any of these approaches might work, but each requires a different flow of logic.

5. Direction

To an important extent, your logic decision will dictate your decision on direction. Still, direction should be a thoughtful part of your message planning. Simply stated, you must now decide where you'll begin and where you'll end your message. If, for example, you've decided to review the past five years' net income, you must now decide whether you'll start off with a discussion of the current year or with a review of the first year under consideration (such as five years ago).

Having made that decision, you must decide where you'll end your discussion. Although the decision about where to end will be greatly influenced by where you decide to start, it's erroneous to think that it will be automatic. Look at the example below.

Example
You're writing a feasibility study of a new mining venture in the Rocky Mountains. You've elected to begin your discussion

with an analysis of the marketplace. If the venture is a coal mine, you've decided to discuss the burgeoning use of coal in power plants, the governmental emphasis on using coal wherever possible. And so on. Still, your ending isn't automatic. You may want to end by discussing projected return on investment. You may want to end by laying out the environmental and governmental blockades to strip mining. You may even want to end by talking about transportation to and from the site. When you select an ending point, however, the large flow of information has been set. All the other information must be fitted into the body of the study.

6. Attitude Toward Reader

Making this decision represents a radical shift in message planning emphasis—away from data and shape and toward style of presentation. You must now decide what your attitude will be toward your reader. There are many options. You can be formal and polite; you can be authoritative; you can be subservient and apologetic; you can be chummy or tyrannical. You can be an impersonal representative of your company, or you can be an old friend who happens to work for your company. The possibilities are limited only by the boundaries of your originality.

Sound a little too premeditated? It may sound that way when first voiced, but actually this decision is the honest crux of your delivery. If you can't determine what your relationship is to the reader, you'll have trouble deciding what your attitude should be. There's real strategy involved. Consider two approaches taken by two different people to the same problem:

Example A
Jane LeDuc has to write a reprimand to one of her employees; the reprimand will be included in the employee's permanent portfolio in personnel. The employee in question has been repeatedly insubordinate. Jane decides to write the reprimand from the following position: "Management has directed me to speak to you about your behavior of August 9." There are several advantages, the chief being that the onus is shifted from Jane to an amorphous group of important (but impersonal) people above her. Jane seems simply to be the tool of her superiors.

Example B
Donald Kortebein decides to write to an insubordinate employee from an entirely different stance. He begins,

"Although I have spoken to you several times about your attitude in this department, I have decided that your behavior yesterday warrants stronger action. I am providing the personnel department with a copy of this memo, and a copy will be held in your records. I am worried that your attitude may severely limit your future in this department, and perhaps with the company. . . ." Donald has chosen an entirely different approach to the message. He has chosen an attitude toward his reader that is straightforward, blunt, and hard-hitting.

Neither Jane's nor Donald's approach is recommended for all situations. The point we're making is that each represents a well-thought-out attitude toward the reader. Jane's attitude is one of an intermediary; Donald's is one of a scolding authority figure with a big stick. Either attitude may work, and both carry the essential explicit warnings. The differences are the authors' varying styles and attitudes.

7. Personal Impression

When you made your attitude decision just now, you decided what you thought about your reader. Now you must decide the other side of the proposition: what you want the reader to think of you. Obviously the two are closely related, but they aren't the same thing. Look back for a minute at the examples of Jane LeDuc and Donald Kortebein. Both have a variety of choices at this decision point. Jane, for instance, has decided to act the role of a go-between, relaying the demands of management to the wayward employee. It's a common decision in such a predicament, but Jane's personal impression options are surprisingly many. They include:

1. The impression of her as a sympathetic supervisor who simply can no longer shield the offending employee.
2. The impression that she has already despaired of improving the performance of the employee in question, and that he is now under the all-seeing eye of corporate big brother.
3. The impression that she isn't fully in accord with the reprimand that management has dictated.
4. The impression that, had the whole matter been left to her, the outcome would have been more (or less) severe.

These are widely different impressions that compose the array of possibilities. For Jane to transfer her meaning most effectively to her insubordinate subordinate, she must choose one of these (or another not listed) and stick to it. Her phrasing of each might read something like the following:

1. "Although I have told my superiors that I feel you have the ability and the willingness to alter your behavior, they have decided . . ."
2. "Because all of our previous counseling sessions seem to have failed, I have turned the whole matter over to . . ."
3. "The action taken by management may seem harsh to us in this department, and I might have preferred to take less drastic action. Nevertheless . . ."
4. "Despite my recommendation that immediate action be taken, management has decided to give you another chance . . ."

The differences must be obvious, even at first examination. And these different attitudes and impressions are (or should be) deliberate, not whimsical. They don't simply evolve from Jane's writing; they're the result of a carefully planned (or premeditated) decision.

The Inevitable Chore: Outlining

Outlining always meets a certain resistance from people who write as part of their everyday living. It seems to be both time-consuming and nonproductive, simply an extra step that takes time, energy, and enthusiasm away from the task at hand: producing the finished document. Why then does every teacher, every trainer, every writing text spend so much time talking about these message skeletons?

Outlines are essential to good writing, and there's no way around it. Good reports, good letters, good memos don't merely happen; they're planned. You wouldn't try to build a house without a blueprint; you shouldn't try to write without an outline. But outlining doesn't have to be the odious, time-consuming chore it was when you learned it in elementary school. It should be exactly the opposite; it should act as a continuing stimulus to your writing. If that's so, what kind of outline will suffice? Basically, you can use any type of outline that will order your thoughts, allocate your space, and ensure that all the important details are included in the right places. It needn't be formal, although (as we'll discuss in chapter 7) a formal outline can be of distinct benefit in organizing a lengthy document.

What must be included? Basically, an outline is just a careful arrangement of the storage-level particles of meaning you want to convey. Let's say, for instance, that you've compiled in your objectives the following list of storage-level particles (and remember that they're in no particular order yet):

1. Client should contact me.
2. Our thermostats are more dependable than anyone else's.
3. Let's look at a sample installation in the area.
4. Our delivery time is virtually immediate.
5. Our prices are competitive.
6. Client's needs are right up our alley.
7. Energy-saving devices are built in.
8. Service is local and fast.
9. System can be upgraded later.
10. We'll provide technical support for related components.

What you're writing is a client proposal for the sale of thermostats for a new hospital installation currently on the drawing boards. Obviously, the order that the particles are in now isn't ideal. As any salesman knows, item number one ("Client should contact me") should be the final and most important element in the proposal, and it appears first on this list. Let's say the following things have already happened in the strategy decisions:

Format:	Proposal
Length—general:	Five pages
Method/organization:	Analysis of client needs fitted to the features of our product
Logic:	Deal with client installations by geographical district
Direction:	Begin with client; end with "client should contact me"
Attitude toward reader:	Friendly, professional
Personal image:	Helpful, well-informed, supportive

Given these decisions, we might develop the following outline by rearranging the storage-level particles:

1. Client's needs are right up our alley.
2. Let's look at a sample installation in the area.
3. We'll provide technical support for related components.
4. Our thermostats are more dependable than anyone else's.
5. Our delivery time is virtually immediate.
6. Our prices are competitive.
7. Service is local and fast.

8. Energy-saving devices are built in.
9. System can be upgraded later.
10. Client should contact me.

How have we applied the decisions? Basically, we've begun the proposal with a discussion of the client's needs and of our product and services in an overall view. Then we've detailed the important subtopics (delivery, price, service). We've concluded with a forward-looking view (energy-saving, the ability to upgrade later on). We've closed with a request for a commitment from the potential client ("If you like what you've read, give me a call").

At this point in time, this ten-point outline is sufficient to fill our needs. No further agony is needed. It's a simple process, easily and quickly done—but it provides an indispensable organizing factor for the important document we're going to generate. If we stick to this outline, we'll cover all the important topics, in a logical order, with proper emphasis on the client (always relating each item back to number one). How can we fail?

Tactics

The final decisions—the tactical decisions—are more detailed. But they're generally easier to make, and will be dictated to a large extent by the outline we've just compiled. By the time we've made these decisions, we'll be ready to write.[1] The first one is closely related to the outline itself, and we've called it a decision on evidence.

1. Evidence

Now that we've decided what particles we want to transfer and store and what order we'll put them in for maximum effect, we have to decide what evidence we'll use to hammer them in. Look at a couple of the sections of the outline we just put together on the thermostat proposal—and the sorts of evidence we might use:

"We'll provide technical support for related components."
a. conduits
b. furnaces/air-conditioning units
c. energy sources
d. governmental regulations

---

1. *Just as a matter of logistics, it's a practical idea when working on a lengthy document to put your outline on index cards, or separate pieces of paper. One topic on each card is ideal. That way you'll be able to record your tactical decisions where they'll do you the most good. If your document will be weighted heavily by data or evidence of some kind, this approach is especially helpful.*

e. specialized needs (surgery, medication storage)
f. emergency needs (power failure)

"Our prices are competitive."
a. We beat all competition in recent bids (name some).
b. We service 45 percent of all hospital accounts in the area.
c. We're not afraid of sealed bidding.

When you've completed the evidence decisions, you'll have an outline that will guide you through the entire writing process. As we'll point out later, you've even developed a table of contents and a formal organizing factor for the proposal. The next decision flows naturally out of this one.

2. Length—Specific

This one is easy and quick. You should allot space to each of the major topics you've included in your outline—making sure that the whole proposal still fits in the space you originally decided should do the whole job (see "Strategy: Length—General"). Once you've decided on the evidence you'll use, you should have some idea which sections will run longer than others and which ones can be dealt with quickly. In the case of our pending thermostat proposal, we might allot a half page to each topic except numbers three (full page), five (one sentence), and ten (closing paragraph only). We'll end up with the five-page document we were looking for.

3. Tone

This decision has something in common with the two that follow: all three are focused on the reader. The decisions we make now will directly facilitate (or impede) the transfer of meaning we want to take place. They must be made thoughtfully and carefully—and they must be followed closely later on when you're writing.

What is the tone of a message? It's an expansion on the strategy decisions of attitude toward reader and personal impression. The tone of your writing will tell your reader what you think of him. If you speak to him as an equal, you'll achieve one effect. You can choose to speak as a superior, as an expert, or as a counselor. If you're writing an apology for a misshipment to an important client, you'll adopt a different tone than you would if you were writing a position paper on offshore drilling.

There are two important rules in making your tone decision:
1. Never use sarcasm in any situation—whether it's intended to be funny or pointed. Sarcasm alienates even people who aren't

involved in the joke. It's tasteless, weak-minded, and offensive. Its epithet as "the last resort of an inferior intellect" is appropriate.
2. When faced with a technical subject with which your reader isn't familiar, never "talk down" to him. If a choice must be made between mystifying your reader and insulting him, opt for mystery. It's no sin to talk over your reader's head occasionally. He may be confused by it (in which case he can ask for clarification), but he shouldn't be offended (unless it's obvious that you're trying to confuse him). In terms of the communication path—he may not store all of your message, but at least he won't store a negative reaction to you. Some people may even be mildly complimented that you thought they'd understand what you said. It's a good idea to follow up a technical discussion with a request for feedback ("I hope I explained that well enough; I apologize for having to include such a technical answer."). No need to go on at length about it, but let the reader know you'd welcome questions.

Remember that your tone decision is simply the manner in which you've decided to implement your strategy decisions of attitude toward reader and personal impression. It shouldn't be a difficult decision when you glance back at those two earlier, guiding decisions. And if you are aware of it—constantly aware of it—you should have no trouble carrying out the decisions you make here.

4. Diction/Jargon

Now that you've determined the tone of your message, you must decide what kind of vocabulary you'll use. If you're an engineer writing to an engineer, you can use all the arcane jargon that's widely understood in your profession. However, if you're an engineer writing to an accountant, you'll have to use a standard dictionary.

Some professions are saturated with jargon; in those cases the task of the writer in making this decision is much more complicated. If you're a systems analyst writing to a user who wants you to write a computerized payroll program, you'll end up as much a translator as a writer. He'll be at a loss to understand what you mean by masterfile, exception reports, batch totals, faulty I/O, or record balancing. You'll have to put those ideas in English if you want your message to be stored properly. (If, on the other hand, you want to ask him to leave everything to your discretion, you may want to puzzle him a bit—who knows?) If you must introduce jargon into a discussion with a layman, be certain that you define it well enough for him to understand it, and that you surround it with plain, everyday words.

5. Attitude Toward Topic

The last decision involves your attitude toward what you're writing about. In the case of the thermostat sale, the writer's attitude toward the topic should convey his feeling that it's an important account—one worth considerable effort. There are situations where the opposite is true. When contacting a colleague about a minor problem, you may well want to de-emphasize its importance:

Charlie:
Just a quick note to remind you that I'll be out all afternoon Friday. Sorry to bother you, but we'd probably do best to meet that A.M. to settle phone coverage while I'm out.

Thanks. Frank

There's a limited range of attitudes that might be taken in the normal course of business. But we've put this decision last because it sometimes acts as an energizer—a galvanizer to the message sender. If your last decision reinforces what you already know about the importance of the message, maybe you'll throw everything you've got into writing.

A Last Word About Decisions

The process we've talked about in this chapter is indispensable to good communication. Obviously, it needn't be as formal as we've sketched it. But it should be conscious. Don't delegate these important decisions to your secretary. Don't hurry past them. You needn't write them all down for unimportant documents. But the more aware you are of what you're saying and of how you're saying it, the more aware your reader is likely to be.

Exercises

1. The decisions for several communications are given in this exercise. Discuss what is inconsistent and how it could be corrected.
   Objective: get employees to give blood
   Strategy:
       format—memo
       length—1 to 1½ pages
       organization—how harmless it is
                   who gains
                   mechanics of blood drives
       logic—personal impression as blood-drive chairman

direction—begin with how easy it is; end with how little
time it takes
attitude toward reader—as an equal
personal impression—sympathetic supervisor
outline—easy to use, who gains by employee giving blood,
how a blood drive works, how little time it takes
to give blood

*In each of exercises 2 through 6, an objective is given. Make a
list of strategy decisions. Include possible alternatives in each.*

2. Request for information on a new real estate development.
3. Response to a written complaint about one of your employees.
4. Request for refund of money paid for unused travel ticket.
5. Clarification of order from customer.
6. Summary description of insurance program.
7. For problems 2 through 6, determine the tactical decisions.
   Indicate how the strategic decisions impacted the tactical
   decisions.
8. You've been asked to determine the management reporting
   requirements for the international operations of your bank.
   As part of your study, you'll be considering the data obtained
   from the bank's current minicomputer system operational
   overseas. Assuming the objectives are to specify data requirements, to discuss the current system, and to recommend an action plan, what strategic decisions would you
   make?
9. Here are several examples of jargon. Discuss what they mean
   and the contexts in which they'd be understood and
   misunderstood.
   a. The modems are strapped together the same way.
   b. It can't transmit, but it will take garbage.
   c. SCS-18 eliminates disk fragmentation and maximizes
   DASD space usage efficiency.
   d. The mailing list system exemplifies the skeletal systems
   that can be created without custom work.
10. You're going to write a letter to a manufacturer about a faulty
    hand drill you purchased. Discuss the pros and cons of
    different decisions with regard to:
    a. attitude toward reader   c. tone
    b. personal impression   d. attitude toward topic
11. We've indicated that you probably make the decisions we
    discussed in this chapter in an automatic way. Take two
    letters or memos you've written and analyze the decisions
    you made in each case. Were the decisions consistent?

Part 3
Four Important Media

6
Letters and Memos

he most common documents in business are letters and memos, and therein lies a problem. As every office worker knows, today's business world is awash in an ever-rising torrent of excess paper. And in dealing with the subject of written communication, we cannot avoid dealing with the problem of unnecessary documents.

We're accustomed to thinking of governmental agencies as prime consumers of paper and forms—the red tape that politicians are always going to eliminate. But for-profit business bureaucracies are no less culpable than government. One recent survey indicates that fully 70 percent of internal correspondence was considered unnecessary and useless by its recipients in the business world. The trouble is that, as long and hard as we look, we never seem to find the people who are sending all that unnecessary paper. Everyone seems willing to validate the idea that excess paper is prevalent everywhere, but nobody is willing to admit that any of it comes from his office. It may just remain one of the great mysteries of modern business.

Even knowing that useless paper always comes from somewhere else, we seek to instill, as an automatic first step in writing letters and memoranda, an evaluation of the necessity for writing. In short, we want to turn off your hand.

Choosing a Medium

At one time in relatively recent history, a letter or a memo was a good way to get something done. It looked important. Now, however, as we wallow about in junk mail, useless mail, carbon copies of everybody's correspondence to everybody else, bulletins to all employees, and more and more, a letter or a memo is likely to be just another piece of paper to add to the stack. To the bottom of the stack.

In most situations, a letter or memo should be your last alternative. Even if you are a dynamic letter writer, you shouldn't choose a no-feedback alternative until after you have rejected all other possibilities. Obviously there are times when only a written message will do: highly technical material, for instance, doesn't transmit very well in spoken messages.

We're certainly not militating against writing in general. You should, however, be aware of the trade-offs in the choice. When you write, you incur the following losses:

No feedback in real time.
More real time elapses before your message is delivered.
More expense (typing, mailing, postage, mail room, and so on).
Your primary communication mode (speech) is subverted to your writing skills.

You have the following advantages:

Ability to convey detail and/or technical material.
Written record of correspondence.
Scheduling benefits.[1]
Time for premeditation and planning.
Written material can be reviewed; spoken cannot.

There are times when you shouldn't even consider writing. Don't ever write anything, for instance, that you want kept absolutely confidential. Your words lose no validity in a photocopy, and unwise scribblings can come back to haunt you years later. Likewise, don't ever use a written format to "run something up the flagpole to see if anyone salutes it." Trial balloons and harebrained suggestions don't belong on paper. Any document is like a courier in an old war movie. It can fall into the wrong hands. Enough said.

Types of Letters

Let's suppose you have decided to write a letter or memo. Your trade-off analysis has indicated that there's more to be gained than lost in writing. Chances are the letter you'll write falls into one or more of three common types:

---

1. Not only can you write a letter when you have the time for it, but you don't have to be there when your reader receives it. Your time is more your own. Don't forget, however, that it takes more time to write than it does to telephone.

descriptive—a nonevaluative survey of a situation, policy, person, organization, or such

analytic—a document that explains why or how and that may or may not be evaluative

persuasive—a document that asks the reader to do something.

There are other types of letters and memos, but most business correspondence fits one or more of these types. Figures 6.1, 6.2, and 6.3 contain sample suggested outlines for the three types of letters. These outlines are designed to apply to all kinds of business documents and appear perhaps more detailed than you need merely for letters; but they do apply and are very useful for letter writing. We'll be using the same outlines for various documents throughout the book. If you follow the procedures outlined in chapter 5, you should be able to use one of these three outlines to finish up the strategy phase of your decisions. Indeed, deciding which outline to use can sometimes clear up major confusions about emphasis, space allotment, and similar areas of choice.

It's possible that two types of outline may be needed within one document. You may, for instance, write a letter to a client that's both analytic (client's situation) and persuasive (buy our product). You may write letters in which more than one subject is covered. In these cases, the three outlines may be melded together to fit the occasion. Look at the letter in figure 6.4; it combines the analytic and persuasive outlines into a single document. The three outlines are not meant to be marble edifices that are unchangeable and unchanging. They are meant to be malleable, flexible, useful concepts to help organize your writing efforts.

Figure 6.1. Descriptive outline.

This five-step descriptive outline can be used for any nonevaluative, descriptive document. Examples of such documents include: geographical surveys, qualitative judgments of places or things, statements about established policies, descriptions of people, descriptions of systems. The outline consists of:

1. Introduction
2. Overview I
3. Specifics
4. Overview II
5. Summary/Conclusion

What do you do in each of these steps? To explain:

1. Introduction. State your reasons for describing: "As you asked, here is a brief description of the new fuel supply system." Explain who you are (if necessary), and tell the familiarity you have with the subject you're describing: "As you know, I have visited the factory only twice now, but I have examined the new system thoroughly on both occasions." Give your credentials: "I studied fuel supply systems while I was at the Northridge plant."

2. Overview I. Try to convey a picture of the whole subject, beginning with whatever are its most dominant characteristics. In describing a person, you might give data about sex, age, height, and hair. It gives the reader an image to work with, to relate specifics to. Keep this overview brief, because the reader will have to keep it all in mind while listening to or reading the next section.

3. Specifics. This is the nitty-gritty. Here you attempt to convey the necessary specifics. Be sure you organize them in some type of system: describe from left to right, from top to bottom, or from beginning to end, so your listener or reader will be able to catalog what you say and fit it into the image he received in the overview.

4. Overview II. Here you reorient the reader to the object as a whole, relating such things as: how the parts fit together, the functions of the whole system. Remember that you are describing a whole something, not just a bunch of separate parts—and the last impression your reader has should be of a whole something.

5. Summary/Conclusion. Relate back to your introduction, and let your reader know just how you have satisfied your goals in describing.

Figure 6.2. Analytical outline.

This five-step outline may be used for any document that answers one or more of the questions: why? how? to what extent? which (of many)? Examples include: technical explanations of machinery or systems, budget justifications, instruction manuals, recommendations, problem-solving explorations. This outline includes:

1. Introduction
2. Situation
3. Method
4. Analysis
5. Conclusion/Recommendation

What to include in each step:

1. Introduction. State your reasons for analyzing, your identity (if necessary), the familiarity you have with your subject, and your credentials.

2. Situation. Give a brief description of the subject of your analysis, with a summary of the needs for analysis. The description should follow the pattern set up in Figure 6.1 (overview-specifics-overview). In this sense, the descriptive outline may be considered a possible subset of this outline.

3. Method. Explain fully the ways you'll analyze the situation displayed in step 2. Enumerate the criteria you'll use, and justify your choices of criteria. Lay out the order in which your analysis will proceed: where it will begin and where it will end. This step necessitates particular attention to the following strategic decisions: method/organization, logic, and direction. Without this guide, your reader may well have substantial trouble following your analysis. It's essential that he know what to expect in the way of technique and level of technical knowledge required. A glossary may be appropriate at this step.

4. Analysis. Apply the methods and criteria you've explained in step 3 to the situation described in step 2. Don't pull any rabbits out of hats, because you will disturb the orderly flow of thought. Use active verbs in short sentences here, and be certain that each sentence flows into the one that follows it. This section may make up as much as three-quarters of the pages in the document.

5. Conclusion/Recommendation. Apply the reasons stated in step 1 to the analysis in step 4. Be certain to indicate any further work that must be done: "My analysis has concentrated heavily on product quality; someone should do more work on the budgetary considerations." If you don't pay attention to the shortcomings of your method, you may be accused (rightfully) of being one-sided or shortsighted.

Figure 6.3. Persuasive outline.

This five-step outline may be used for any argumentative or persuasive document. Examples include: sales materials, political or lobbying materials, customer-service materials, requests for budget increases, suggestions for changes in policy or procedures.

1. Introduction/Attention
2. Statement of Need

3. The World Without the Need
4. Solution
5. Required Action

What to do:

1. Introduction/Attention. How you do this is a matter of individual style; what you must do is motivate the reader to read on. What you must do as well is fully identify yourself and your pertinent affiliations. You may find it useful to mention credentials, mutual friends, or mutual concerns.

2. Statement of Need. Pinpoint the need you'll attempt to satisfy with your solution. Don't mention the solution, even though it may be obvious from the letterhead or from your identity. This section must be based solidly on statements concerning the reader; it must make him aware of a pressing need. It must also make him aware of your knowledge of that need and of his situation.

3. The World Without the Need. Picture for your reader what his world would be like without the need established in step 2. Don't mention your solution. You must strive for a commitment from your reader at this point. If you can get him to agree with this utopian vision, you're well on your way to a successful argument. Be sure to employ the descriptive outline in figure 6.1 in describing the world without need.

4. Solution. This section is recognizable as a sales pitch. You explain how your solution alone can solve the reader's problem (step 2) and bring him to the world described in step 3. If your solution is lengthy or technical, you may find it necessary to employ steps 2, 3, and 4 from the analytical outline presented in figure 6.2. At any rate, what you must do is build your solution into the trouble-free world you constructed above. You must get a commitment from the reader at this point to proceed to the final step.

5. Required Action. Tell the reader the very next step he must take to get to the world as described in step 3: "Vote for the bond issue," "Give me a call," "Send your check," "Fill out the enclosed coupon." Without a specific required action here, you've wasted your whole document.

Figure 6.4.   Letter combining analytical and persuasive characteristics.

The letter in this figure is intended to summarize the results of a study on several types of reproduction machines and the copier operations within the department.

Dear Mr. Blake:

Introduction   As you know, I have been studying the situation in the Operations Department with respect to duplicating. The study has included interviews with users in the Department, equipment operators, and vendors over the last three weeks.

Attention/   Several major problems have been identified, including 1) complaints about the quality of copies, 2) machines jamming, 3) long delays in getting copies. These problems have resulted in a 10-15% reduction in departmental efficiency. The situation that must be addressed includes 1) office procedures, 2) improved equipment requiring less maintenance and repair, 3) increased copying volume.

World   If these problems can be solved, maintenance without and supply costs can be reduced 70% and need productivity increased by at least 10%.

Method/   The approach in the study was to conduct
Analysis/   extensive interviews, review procedures and
Solution   equipment records, and evaluate vendor documents. Four alternative copiers were evaluated—including A, B, C, and D. Vendor X, which makes copier C, is superior for your needs since it has a better repair record and is cheapest with your volume of work. It also will be easier to operate.

We recommend that you place an order for model C from Vendor X. After installation, the other recommendations or changes in office procedures can be implemented.

Yours truly,

Before we proceed into the decisions you should make to write a letter or memo, a word of caution: letters require more care and craftsmanship than reports. They are much more likely to be read and taken to heart than any other type of document. They must be clear, brief, and attractive, as well as easy to understand, straightforward, and complete. That's a big order.

Objectives

When you compile your objectives, you'll probably be able to place them in one of the outline patterns we've discussed. Note that down. Do you want merely to convey some information to the reader (descriptive)? Do you want to activate him to do something? Are you analyzing something and recommending alternatives?

Remember, when compiling your stated and implied particles of meaning, that people are much more inclined to "read between the lines" in a letter than they are in other media. If you decide to imply anything, take particular care from here on to implement that particle through your strategy and tactics decisions. Here's an example. You're writing a letter to the Employee Relations (ER) representative in Cheyenne, Wyoming. The particles you want stored in your reader's mind are:

Stated
We are closing down operations in Cheyenne.
All employees are being put on layoff status until further notice. It is your duty to inform them and to coordinate their response. We will try to place all employees at other company locations.
Layoff compensation will be as per the Company Procedures
    Manual and will relate to seniority, classification, etc.

Implied
When you finish this dirty work, we'll find a nice, cushy job for
    you in the home office.

The reason that the implied particle is implied is obvious. You're not making any overt promises to a hatchet man. As far as anyone on the outside (or on the inside, for that matter) can see, you're simply going to "place" your ER representative "at other company locations" before the rest of those "on layoff status" can blink. For legal reasons, you don't want to commit to any of that in so many words. For morale reasons, you'd prefer that the implication act as a carrot-and-prod mechanism through the unpleasant time ahead in Cheyenne.

How do you convey the implied particle? You convey it through your answers to the following decision points: attitude toward reader, personal impression, tone. You refer to the layoffs as "they" and to the "placed ones" as "you." You sign the letter in a familiar manner.

Although it's not applicable in the case we've just sketched, the most common form of implication is a simple indication at the foot of a letter that you're sending carbon copies to others. A letter or memo with a carbon to the division vice-president certainly carries an unmistakable implied particle. A mildly worded complaint carries additional weight if it's also sent to the Better Business Bureau and the Consumer Protection Agency. A lot can be done with carbons, but each time you send an unnecessary copy of a letter, you are contributing to the paper flood we talked about earlier.

Strategy

The first two strategy decisions (format and general length) are generally more important to a letter or a memo than they are to a report. Whether you decide to write a two-page letter on your company letterhead or a simple note "from Bill Jones," be aware of the implications of the format and the hidden message in the length decision.

Many companies have fixed policies about correspondence formats but, even within these policies, there's usually some room for judgment. There are times, for instance, when you want a letter to seem more personal than institutional, or when you want your letter to be seen as "off the record." The following is such a situation:

Albert Golding is a salesman for a company of which the principal product line is frozen french-fried potatoes. He has been in contact with the produce buyer from a large fast-food chain; the fellow seems to be a good prospect. Albert's sales pitch has always included a good deal of backslapping and "above and beyond" favors. Albert has decided to send his potential client a packet of information on his french fries—but a packet with a bit more punch than the standard company issue. He includes in it some selections from a national consumer magazine praising his product line. That particular magazine doesn't allow its product evaluations to be used in advertising or marketing—and will take action when it finds that a company violates that rule.

When Albert sends the bundle of clippings to his potential client, he won't accompany it with a formal letter on his company's letterhead. He'll paper-clip a note to the top clipping: "Tony—Here's the information I said I'd drop by. Hope it helps you in your decision. See you next week. Al."

Now, the fact that Albert used a blank memo form instead of the company letterhead accomplished several things:

1. It did not make it seem that what he was doing was on behalf of his employer—or at least not on his employer's instructions.
2. It made it seem that Albert was doing a personal favor for Tony.
3. It enabled Albert to write to Tony legitimately without copying the sales files.

None of these three implications is inconsequential.

When making a decision regarding length, try to avoid lengths of more than two pages. Your average letter should be slightly less than one page long. There's no way that such a rule can be made absolute; there are certain important letters that simply must be quite lengthy. (That proves the old adage about rules being made to be broken. The point to rules—in communication, at least—is that you should be aware when you break them.) The most important consideration in making a decision as to length is, of course, your judgment of the reader's willingness and ability to read your message. Does he have time to read? Does the topic touch him closely enough to motivate him to read? Does he have the technical expertise required to read a full analysis?

A Packet of Small Pieces

There are ways in which some lengthy documents can be handled to yield a group of small documents—an approach that is sometimes preferable for a variety of reasons. Let's examine such a case. Let's say that Linda Green, a sales representative for a mortgage broker, is contacting a client at a pension fund investment department. Linda wants to convince her client that the pension fund can maximize its yield on investment by buying second trust deeds on residential properties.

The subject of second trust deeds is complex and burdened with a considerable amount of governmental regulation: escrows, title searches and policies, flood insurance, installment payment agreements, liens, assessments, and on and on. Linda wants to cover all this territory in her letter, so her client can make a quick and well-informed decision. She knows two important facts about her client:

1. He is interested in high-yield investments, because the pension plan is tax-free. Therefore, traditional tax-free issues like municipal bonds will appear less attractive to him because their chief asset (which is being tax-free) doesn't apply to his situation.
2. He is constantly besieged by people who are offering him investments of various types.

The two facts seem mutually exclusive in their dictates about length. The first seems to indicate that she ought to provide as much information as possible; the second indicates that brevity may be the soul of discretion. What Linda must do is strike a compromise.

One of the prime reasons that sales groups develop and use printed information is to accommodate situations of this type. Linda's best option is to grab a few pamphlets that aptly describe the intricacies and advantages of second trust deeds and to enclose them with a crisply worded, brief sales pitch in the form of a cover letter. The potential client has several options upon receiving such a package of information. He can read it all. He can forward some of it to his colleagues who may have an interest in it. He can file pieces of it for future retrieval. Best of all, he'll probably have plenty of time to read Linda's short appeal.

If you aren't fortunate enough to have a selection of pamphlets you can enclose (or if the pamphlets available are not to your taste—which is frequently the case), you can fake it. How? By creating your own packet of small pieces, organized by category and enclosed as a series of attachments to your letter. Let's assume, for the moment, that Linda doesn't have available a brochure that contains information salient to this particular client's needs. What can she do? First, she should write a one-page letter emphasizing her most important particles of meaning:

1. Second trust deeds are secure investments.
2. Second trust deeds are high-yield investments.
3. Second trust deeds provide extremely liquid investments.

Then she can write a series of short explanations of pertinent issues and attach them as enclosures with the letter. This shows Linda's client that she's aware of his need for information, but that she respects his busy schedule as well.

The approach of sending a packet of small pieces, used over a period of time, also provides the writer with a file of information that can be easily copied and reused in future. And virtually any letter that seems to require great length for effect can be adapted to this procedure. When you come across a letter or memo that doesn't adapt itself easily or without strain, then go ahead—write an epistle. But keep it as unadorned as possible, using short sentences, short paragraphs, and short words.

Method, Logic, and Direction

Since most letters are (or should be) short, these three decision points are frequently combined in practice. They are no less important because they can be clumped together, however.

A letter absolutely requires a sharp, clear beginning and end. In very few (*very* few) cases is an air of mystery appropriate. Your reader should know, within a few words of the beginning of the letter, exactly where you're headed and how you intend to get there. The outlines provided in figures 6.1, 6.2, and 6.3 can usually be used without alteration for letter planning.

There's an old adage that used to be common in business letter writing courses. It is no less apt today than it was fifty years ago: Tell them what you're going to say, then say it, then tell them what you said. If you can do that without being redundant, your letters will have an unarguable clarity.

Attitude and Impression

We discussed the definitions of these two decisions in chapter 5. That discussion should be almost directly applicable to your letter writing. There's a consideration, however, that we should bring out in the open because it's important to think about while you're making these two decisions: the environment within which you write and the reader reads. It would be naivete of the worst sort to pretend that business is not riddled with politics, with environmental burdens that affect virtually everything we write or say in one way or another. Let's take a moment to examine the environment in which business is transacted. We'll look at it as though it were divided into two principal components: the problematic environment and the sustaining environment.[2]

The Problematic Environment

Business life is composed of a series of decisions and problems. Not all the problems are major, but they remain problems. They

---

2. *For a full discussion, see Allen and Lientz,* Systems in Action: A Managerial and Social Approach *(Santa Monica, Calif.: Goodyear, 1978).*

might be the problems of selling a client your goods or services. They might be the problems of explaining a new process to your superiors or to a budget committee. They might be the problems of creating a public relations image that will enhance the standing of your company in the eyes of the media or the marketplace. They might be simply the problems of keeping employees performing at their best.

However you view business, it's a fact that most writing is aimed at solving problems. And those problems are contained in an environment that either causes them or allows them to happen. The components of this problematic environment are myriad. There are legal requirements, personnel requirements, product requirements, financial requirements. But none of them is easily separable from the others.

Once you isolate the problem you want to deal with, you should give some thought to how that problem interlocks with the environment around it. For instance, say you want to write a memorandum to a manager from another department within your company to complain about poor performance by a member of his group. You wouldn't be complaining if that poor performance hadn't caused repercussions in your job. Your job becomes part of the environment of the poor performance. Because your job is affected, so are the jobs of your clients (whether they be inside your company or outside). Because your complaint is related to personnel, you engender a problem relationship with the employee relations group and, through them, with the government and with outside groups such as unions. All these groups, functions, and people are part of the problematic environment for which you're trying to find a solution in your writing.

Make no mistake, every decision you make in business affects a widely dispersed group of people. Each decision is like a pebble dropped in a pool; the ripple effect it causes is the same. Most of those ripples are too small to be felt widely, but they happen nonetheless. They contribute to your working image, your job performance, the way you are viewed by management and by clients. And your understanding of and sympathy with the problematic environment will dictate the extent to which you'll consciously involve it in your writing. No problem exists in a vacuum.

The Sustaining Environment

Contained within the problematic environment, however, must be the seed or the possibility of a solution. In fact, most problems

—even while they remain problems—are dealt with in some fashion. That dealing may be a temporary stalling device, or it may be an old, outmoded solution. Let's take an example.

You've decided to write a memorandum to the manager of customer relations. You just spoke with one of your regular outside clients, who's dissatisfied with a settlement he got from your company on a shipment of defective parts. Your letter to customer relations will be to advise them of your position and to plead for better settlements in future, should similar problems arise.

Your letter, aside from attempting to point out a problem, is part of a temporary solution. Since the system didn't work the way it was supposed to (with the client asking for and getting a settlement that both sides considered to be fair), you're temporizing another solution. What is that solution? Your letter, of course. Your letter is a temporary system that is trying to rectify a lack of communication or a lack of agreement between your client and the customer relations department.

The current environment contains all the components of this temporary solution: you, the client, and customer relations. Although there seems to be an unsolved problem, you're dealing with it in a manner that attempts a solution. You're also trying to create a system that will help avoid similar problems in the future.

The current environment also contains the possibility of other types of solutions. Your client could sue, for example. Your client could take his business elsewhere. Either of those solutions would also deal with the problem.

In the final analysis, you must locate the parts of the current (or problematic) environment that will allow you to create a solution that will eliminate future problems. And that solution must be workable—and compatible with the environment as it will be after the problem is solved. The solution must be sustained by a part of the environment that we call the sustaining environment. The sustaining environment is the part of the problematic environment that sustains improvements in the system.

Your aim in writing should always be to locate and help create a solution compatible with the sustaining environment. Going back into the preceding example, the parts of the environment you'll deal with in trying to create a temporary solution will also be the parts that must eventually reach a permanent solution. If no permanent solution is reached, it may be that the temporary solution (scolding letters) is the best possible permanent solution. If that's so, you must appeal to the parts of the environment that will allow it to continue. That is to say, you should not alienate the customer relations manager because you may need to ask favors of him in the future.

How does all this reflect on the decisions we call attitude toward reader and personal impression? Look back at the example. If you were acting solely on the single case, you might take a hard line with the customer relations group—flay them alive for disrupting a client relationship that's quite profitable for the company. On the other hand, if you're endeavoring to keep your communication open and productive with customer relations, you may want to try something less heavy-handed or authoritarian.

This discussion of environments is in no way advice to soft-pedal everything you write for fear of offending someone. Sometimes offense is the only avenue open. What we are counseling you to do is examine the entire environment, the ripple effects, before you act.

Tactics

As you'll see in the next chapter, the tactics used in reports aim at organizing and presenting data in whatever quantity is sufficient to substantiate your claims or theories. In letter writing, however, the tactics, or evidence decisions, are severely constrained by space. That constraint offers two alternatives, either of which is acceptable, depending on your circumstances. In short, you can either abbreviate the length of each piece of evidence or you can limit the number of pieces of evidence.

In some cases, when the facts are either well-known or easily understood, a simple list of supporting evidence is sufficient. In other cases, you may have to sort through your evidence for the one or two pieces that will be most effective in your particular situation. In a sales presentation, for instance, you may find that using the strongest evidence (and only the strongest evidence) is preferable to swamping your client with information. In other situations, a simple statement of evidence is all that is advisable. If you're firing an employee, for instance, you may want to include a mountain of evidence for legal reasons, but not much description of any one piece.

If you've elected to use the "packet of small pieces" approach, you must be careful to key the brochures to the letter with such statements as this: "As the brochure on collateralized loans makes clear . . ."

The remaining tactics decisions should come fairly simply, as they were described in chapter 5. A couple of hints: the specific-length decisions should be made in units of sentences or paragraphs. The tone and-attitude-toward-topic decisions must take the environment into account as an extension of the strategic decisions of attitude toward reader and personal impression.

Before We Let the Subject Drop

The caution with which we started the chapter is worth repeating. The world is floundering in paperwork generated by bored or frightened (or both) desk workers. Art Buchwald, in the following selection, puts his finger on the cause of one major category. Buchwald's style is amusing, but his subject is deadly serious.

Memo on the Memo on the Memo

By Art Buchwald

President Carter is pledged to cut down paperwork in Washington. Abernathy, a government bureaucrat, says he can't do it.

"It's a question of communication," he said. "There are two ways of communicating in the government—orally and in print. I could communicate verbally with somebody, but no one would be aware that I was doing my job."

"The person you communicated with would know," I said.

"That's not enough," he said. "In government it is essential that as many people as possible are aware that you are working. The only way they can know this is if you send them copies of memoranda that you have originated. The more people there are on your 'need-to-know' list the more important your job with the agency will seem."

"It makes sense," I said, "but surely even these communications could be cut down to achieve Carter's goal."

"They could," said Abernathy, "except that a memo does not have value unless the one who sends it demands a response. What good is a memorandum on an issue until you can get 10 people to comment in writing on it?"

"They probably welcome the opportunity to do it," I said.

"Of course, and this is where the President is up against a wall. Since I originated the memorandum, there is a certain

---

amount of jealousy because it is now known as the 'Abernathy Memo.' The only way the other bureaucrats can get back at me is to respond with a report on the memo that they can then put their names on. For example, Freedman would title his the 'Freedman Report in Answer to the Abernathy Memorandum.' To play catch-up, he would be obligated to circulate this to twice as many people as I did."

"Now you're really getting into paper" I said.

"That's only the beginning, Altshuler would have to top Freedman by calling a meeting at which he would give an audio-visual presentation of his opinions with copies to all those present as well as those who couldn't attend. He would include graphs, statistics and research in various colors. It would be called the 'Altshuler Response to the Freedman Answer on the Abernathy Memorandum.' "

"But suppose you cut the distribution list for memos in half. Wouldn't that cut down the paperwork?"

"It might if status didn't play such an important part in government communications. Suppose you sent a memo to Crosby but left Schuster off the list. Schuster would consider that you were trying to push him out of the picture and retaliate by cutting you off *his* list. It could get very rough because it doesn't pay to have Schuster as an enemy, particularly when he could sabotage you in the dining room by saying he saw your memo to Crosby and it made no sense at all."

"I can see where that wouldn't work," I said.

"You have another problem," Abernathy said. "It's dangerous to send out a memorandum in the government because by doing so you're sticking your neck out. But if you can comment on *somebody else's* memo, you're in a safe position because you weren't the originator of the idea.

"If you cut people off your list and they start cutting you off their distribution list you will be forced to write more *original* memos that eventually will get you in trouble. Harper, who used to work in the next office did this. He only sent his memos to two people. He got so few memos in return that they decided he didn't have enough to do and they fired him."

Abernathy said, "The only way you can measure productivity in the government is by how much paperwork a person is producing. If he has nothing in his files, there is no way the President knows he's doing his job."

"Is Mr. Carter aware of this?"

"Yes, I just sent him a long memorandum on it this morning."

Exercises

In each of problems 1 through 5, you are to write a paragraph that takes the reader from the familiar to the unfamiliar aspects of the subject.

1. subject—computer payroll system
   your reader—manual payroll system clerk
2. subject—dictating machine
   your reader—supervisor
3. subject—overhead projector
   your reader—potential speaker
4. subject—job application form
   your reader—potential applicant
5. subject—photocopying machine
   your reader—new secretary
6. For each of problems 1 through 5, suppose you're in marketing and that you want to write a brief sales statement on the object, directed to the same reader. In each case compare it with the result in the first exercise with problems 1 through 5.
7. Look around your desk and find three letters or memos that shouldn't have been sent. What are their shortcomings? Could anything have been done to prevent failure? What other message could have been conveyed?

In problems 8 through 11, a situation is given. Discuss the pros and cons of whether to write a letter.

8. A department store has overcharged you $84.13.
9. You object strongly to an editorial in a local paper.
10. You have compiled a new book that would be a useful reference for eight other people in your department.
11. You have just received a memorandum that is critical of a report you completed recently.
12. In problems 8 through 11, identify the various audiences in terms of what has been discussed in the chapter.
13. In problems 8 through 11, discuss what could go wrong with the letter. How could it become a smoking pistol?

In each of exercises 14 through 17, develop a descriptive, analytic, or persuasive outline.

14. operating instructions for a toaster
15. project report for a project behind schedule
16. write-up of your department's two-year operating plan
17. memo on the use of the new training room

In each of exercises 18 through 20, identify what's wrong in terms of the outline being followed and audience being addressed.

18. Important. You need to read to familiarize yourself with our new overdue book policy. Books in category A will be charged at 15¢ per day. Books in category B will be charged 10¢ per day up from 5¢. Children's books are still 2¢ per day. We hope you will adhere to this policy.

19. To: Managers and Supervisors
    From: Regis Reed, Vice-President
    Subject: Unauthorized use of envelopes

    It has come to my attention that we have had a shrinkage of envelopes. Since our mailing expenses are not increasing noticeably, it is apparent that envelopes are disappearing. We checked this information several times over the last two months. We hope you will conserve envelopes to help the company reduce its costs. Thank you for your cooperation.

20. Dear Sir:
    I want to introduce you to our new municipal bond investment fund. The fund is composed of securities rated A to AAA. The current annual yield is 6.2%. The income is free of federal income taxes and is partially free of certain local taxes. Analysis shows that it is a suitable investment for individuals in the 38% federal tax bracket. We hope you will read the attached brochure and call us at your convenience.

7

Reports

Like all worthwhile business documents, reports serve two purposes. First, they organize and convey timely information; second, they constitute official entries into the corporate memory. They're widely used as reference documents and thus may acquire an aura of authority that may not be warranted.

The need for reports is (or should be) encountered less often than the need for letters and memos. And, when a report is required, compiling it and drafting it can be a puzzling and bothersome assignment. The job of report writing is made no more easy by the fact that reports are seldom credited to a single individual; they're usually seen as the collective product of a group of people. If a good report bears a signature, it's generally the signature of the manager in charge—not of the real report writer.

There are several corporate needs that require reporting documents. The most common one—and the most important—is the solution or analysis of a problem. Such a problem can be part of any of the three main areas of management decision making:

tactical decision making: relatively short range, data generated
　　from inside sources
managerial decision making: medium range, data generated both
　　from inside and outside sources
strategic decision making: long range, data generated largely
　　from outside sources

The investigation, data-gathering, analysis, and recommendation of alternatives is frequently documented in a formal report.

Another frequently requested report is called a *white paper*, which asks for or states policy positions on specific questions.

That policy may be simply a statement of clarifying information, but more commonly it relates to the public interface of the corporation: the government, the media, the public, the financial establishment.

Other common reports include:

1. the *periodic report:* a regularly published document (weekly, monthly, yearly) that usually deals with such topics as resources consumed, major events that have occurred, forward planning, routine accomplishments

2. the *status (or progress) report:* a document surveying the currency of a project that usually contains a discussion of schedule, milestones, and budget

3. the *meeting report:* a circulated summary of topics covered in a meeting which usually is not as comprehensive as formal minutes, but notes resolutions, decisions, tasks assigned, and so forth.

Reports are ridden with jargon and with "in" references. There's no way around that, because one assumes that the reader of a report must have enough interest in and knowledge of the subject to want to read. But the fact that readers are qualified by job interest does not remove the writer's task of writing to the audience. And writing to the audience implies a good working knowledge of the audience.

Figure 7.1 lists some questions you should ask yourself about each segment of the audience. You can apply the questions to a particular person or to a theoretical reader who represents a larger audience.[1] The questions are grouped into three categories: the reader, you and the reader, and the reader's response. Under each category there are a number of more specific questions. Answering the first group of questions helps you determine who (or where) the reader is. The answers are directed to the general background of the audience. The second group pins down the reader's attitude toward the writer and the subject matter. Answers to these questions lead us to predicting the reader's likely response and future feedback. No absolute determinations can be made, of course—to try to second-guess your reader is foolhardy 98 percent of the time—but you can orient both your writing and your expectations to a reasonable reader's response. The third group tries to do just that.

---

1. *And don't forget that one potential reader of virtually all reports is the government in its many apparitions: IRS, Justice, Commerce, Labor, courts, and on and on.*

Figure 7.1. Questions to identify your reader.

General: What is the background of your reader?
Specific: What is the formal, organizational relationship?
             What was the previous formal relationship?
             How much time will the reader have for your report?
             What is the reader's preference regarding the organization, tone, and style of presentation?
General: What is the quality of your relationship with the reader?
Specific: What is the informal relationship?
             How long have you known the reader?
             What is the reader's attitude toward you?
             What is the reader's attitude toward the subject?
General: What is the reader's response likely to be?
Specific: How long will the response take to be sent and received?
             What is your next likely step after receiving the response?
             Can these later communications be eliminated or can the time for communication be compressed?

Reports Versus Letters

Reports are different from letters in many ways. They aren't as strictly constrained by length; they're frequently constrained quite heavily by established format. A corporate memory needs to store information in formats that make it retrievable by an established method. In other words, anyone browsing through the files should be able to read and interpret the data in your report. Over a period of time, most corporations develop reporting styles that become matters of policy.

Although reports follow the same decision process as letters, the decisions are more detailed and the emphases are different. Reports are more complex because of:

1. the amount of data collection they require
2. the extent of the analysis they include
3. their use of visual aids to display technical material

On top of that, a report writer is usually required to prepare a one-page summary of the report. This summary is frequently persuasive, even though the report itself is analytic or descriptive.

After all, who wants to go to a lot of effort without recommending some kind of change or improvement?

Pitfalls

What causes a report to be received, filed, and forgotten? Why might a single problem be studied and restudied many times without action? In western Los Angeles, there are a series of canals (Venice) that have decayed from sixty years of neglect. The money spent on successive studies would have paid for implementing any one of the alternative actions suggested in the first study.

The reports on the Venice canals didn't generate enough support to acquire a constituency and command action. If you write a report with general or vague recommendations, you may end up with a general, vague endorsement of the report—instead of a specific action plan. Figure 7.2 lists some other reasons for failure.

Figure 7.2.   Why reports fail.

Conclusions/ Recommendations

appeal to competing
   audiences
too general and long-term
too short-range without
   long-term plan
unrealistic in terms of
   resources needed to carry
   them through

Data Collection

incomplete
overdone, report is late
made from poor choice of
   sources

Analysis

uses data improperly
draws wrong conclusions
   from data
uses nonstandard methods
   that aren't acceptable
length and ponderousness
   causes message to be lost
doesn't cover the effects of
   implementing the
   recommendations

Defining the Project

To analyze the project initially, you'll need to know:

1. Why is the project important?
2. Who is the user or receiver of the report?

3. What has been done before?
4. What deadlines are present?
5. Where will data be collected? From whom?
6. What are potential solutions to the problem?
7. What analysis techniques are likely to be needed?

Let's consider some of these questions in more detail.

1. Why is the report important? Or, what is the goal? Is it merely to collect and disseminate information? Is it to analyze and make recommendations for change? If it's the latter, you need to collect sufficient data to argue from the position of an expert (refer back to chapter 4 to review the various types of arguments).
2. Who is the user or receiver of the report? You must be sensitive to the characteristics of the audience members, including:
    a. their reporting relationship to you (superior, external, not related)
    b. their technical background and interest
    c. their sympathy or commonality of interest
    d. their potential reaction to your writing.
3. What has been done before? Look around. Has a similar problem been written up? With what result? Can you use the ideas or the approach from the previous work? You might look for reports in other departments with similar problems. If you're doing a routine report, then you can use a standard form. But don't be afraid to be innovative. Preparing a new report in a better way may help you.
4. What are the deadlines? This question relates to the scope or extent and depth of the report as well as to its importance. Answering this question gives you an idea of how much effort you'll spend on it and its priority on your time.

A frequent problem is limiting the scope to the time available to prepare the report and to the time and inclination of the audience to get through the report. Beware—if the scope is too broad and time is short, it's likely that the report will be hastily written and will fail. Let's consider an example.

You're assigned to compare and recommend among several spare-parts suppliers. You have one week to do it. You first determine what has been done before and who the audiences are. Then you grapple with the scope. It turns out there are five suppliers in town. A visit to a supplier takes over five hours—you can only get through one per day. You decide how much time you need to write the report and have it typed. Let's say that the writing and typing will take two days. Since you have one week to do the report, your scope is limited to three suppliers.

You haven't begun collecting data and you already need to pin down the scope of solutions and analysis methods. Where do you get answers to these questions? Normally, you get them from the person who asked you to do the project.

In real life, there are external factors that impact how a project will be treated. This is something most books don't mention; they assume you'll just plunge ahead. But wait! Before you commit to responding to someone's request, you must check its priority relative to other projects. There are also political factors to consider. If the requester is important and his request isn't, you may still want to do it first. In any event, you need to lay out a schedule for accomplishing your objective.

The Problem Report

Writing a problem report requires definition of the problem in addition to your project definition. The same questions, slightly refined, apply: What kind of problem is the report investigating? Why is it a problem and why is the problem important? Is the goal to treat the problem? To alter its effects? To avoid it? Or to eradicate its causes? Who's affected by the problem? Who'll benefit by its solution? Who might *lose* benefit because of its solution? Are there deadlines inherent in the problem? For example, is it getting worse? How fast? Can it generate further problems if it isn't solved?

It's a good idea to look at an overall approach to problem solving before beginning a report on a problem. After all, you're probably being asked to solve the problem itself, as well as report on it. Because of that, we've adapted a skeletal problem-solving approach to the task of report writing. The simple diagram presented in figure 7.3 sets out the steps a careful report writer takes. As you contemplate the diagram, note carefully the reverse arrows. They indicate points at which you should consider the impact of current work on previous research. If you observe the negative arrows, you'll avoid the trap of making unsupported or insufficiently supported claims.

Let's assume you've investigated the problem somewhat or that you've been assigned a report by someone who has investigated the problem. ("Johnson, I want you to write up what happened last Friday at the factory and tell me what ought to be done about it.") Once you have a general idea of the problem, you proceed to the step labeled "collect the data."

Figure 7.3. Steps in Report Writing

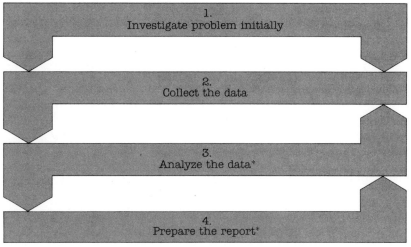

*The reverse arrows indicate feedback to the previous stage.

Collecting Data

You want to get going. Time is pressing. You need to collect data. Right? But stop. Sit back. You need a framework to make collecting and analyzing data easier.

Defining a Framework

That framework consists of the following general elements:

1. Introduction
    a. Why is this being written?
    b. What's the problem?
    c. What's the scope of the approach?
    d. What are the data sources?
2. Central part
    a. What's the approach?
    b. How will the findings and analysis be organized?
    c. How will they be presented?
3. Wrap-up
    a. What's the form of the recommendation?
    b. To what degree will you discuss implementation of the recommendations?

Notice that these words are casual. That's intended; this isn't an outline. Making an outline now might tend to limit your later efforts—fence you in. You want the framework to serve—not vice versa. The framework helps you define the problem, the objectives and purpose, the approach, and the way you handle the results of your work.

You may recall that in our example you're going to identify a supplier of spare parts for your organization. Let's take a cut at the framework.

1. Introduction
   a. why—present supplier of spare parts is deficient
   b. what—identify a cost-effective supplier of spare parts
   c. scope—five days are available, three sources of spare parts can be contacted
   d. source—the relationship with the present supplier; three external potential sources
2. Central part
   a. approach (how?)—data collected by interview with suppliers, internal employees, and current users of supplier
   b. organization—statement of problem, pros and cons of each alternative supplier, evaluation
3. Wrap-up
   a. form of recommendation—recommend a supplier
   b. implementation—steps needed to set up an account with supplier

Notice that we didn't define our evaluation criteria, nor did we prejudge the supplier. Now you're ready to start collecting data.

There are several approaches to doing a report. Each involves a different collection of sources. You can search a library or departmental reference file. You can take direct observations. You can conduct experiments. Figure 7.4 lists some of the general references useful in report preparation.

Figure 7.4.   Useful references.

1. **On locating information**
   Reader's Guide to Periodical Literature
   Business Periodicals Index
   Wall Street Journal Index
   New York Times Index
   Social Science and Humanities Index
   Education Index

2. **General factual information**
   Random House College Dictionary
   Encyclopedia Americana
   Encyclopaedia Britannica
   The World Almanac and Fact Book
   Fortune Dictionary
   Rand McNally World Atlas
   Bureau of the Census publications, particularly the Statistical Abstract of the United States
   A Dictionary of Slang and Unconventional English, by E. Partridge
   Bartlett's Quotations

3. **Biography**
   Who's Who in America (and a variety of sub–Who's Whos by geographic areas, industries, and professions)

4. **Report style and format**
   A Manual of Style (University of Chicago Press)
   A Manual for Writers of Term Papers, Theses, and Dissertations, by Kate L. Turabian (University of Chicago Press)

5. **Data bank sources**
   New York Times Information Bank
   Lockheed Corporation
   System Development Corporation (SDC)
   Stanford Research Institute (SRI)

Questionnaires

Formal data collection is frequently done on questionnaires. Questionnaires require work in design, preparation, sampling, and handling responses. Figure 7.5 presents some suggestions regarding questionnaires. Part of the bottom line of their use is statistical validity. You must present information that indicates the validity of your survey.[2]

2. *For a discussion of interviewing techniques—which may also be useful in completing report data—see chapter 9, "Oral Presentations."*

Figure 7.5. Suggestions on questionnaires.

1. Questionnaires should be avoided if there are easier, more reliable ways of obtaining data available.
2. Questionnaires require a great deal of effort in preparation and analysis.
3. Steps in planning and preparation include:
   a. Keep audience in mind in determining the length and terminology of questionnaire.
   b. Avoid words and phrases that might bias responses; avoid leading questions.
   c. Aim for clarity and avoid ambiguity in wording.
   d. Pretest the questionnaire on a very small sample that's representative of a larger sample.
   e. Accompany and, if possible, precede the questionnaire by a letter (builds anticipation for questionnaire).
   f. Tell the respondents what they can expect in the way of feedback—usually a summary of results.
   g. Follow up the questionnaire with postcards to encourage response or to thank respondents for their replies.
4. What can be done to increase the response rate?*
   a. Precede and follow up the mailing with telephone calls to identify the recipient precisely.
   b. Send the questionnaire by first-class mail.
   c. Use a personalized letter with a prestigious letterhead.
   d. Hand sign each letter.
   e. Professionally print and send the questionnaire.

*There is something in common about all of these—they take time and/or money. You'll need to do trade-off analysis to determine which of these to do.

Computers

Computer technology has impacted data collection. Questionnaires are now frequently designed for keypunch and data entry into a computer system. In addition to this, we can use the computer to get access to commercial or subscription data bases. A data base is a repository of data compiled on a particular subject. Some kinds of data bases are:

1. Economic.
2. Census.
3. Industry.
4. Building codes and permits.

These data bases are available from various computer time-sharing services, including Data Resources Inc. Once you have a computer terminal and a valid contract, you can dial into the service, select the data base from a name, and then specify data elements you want. The data you select can then be processed through statistical and graphic capabilities offered by the service. These packages perform the following functions: basic statistics and tabulation, advanced statistics (such as regression analysis, analysis of variance, and factor analysis), and graphic and tabular output. You have the capability of formatting output with the scale, headings, and legend you want so it can be copied directly for presentation.

Analyzing the Data

Although the sequence we have used here indicates that this step occurs after the data has been collected, that is not always the case. The process is reiterative (see figure 7.2).

Assemble all your notes and organize them. For example, in the supplier case, you've collected data from three suppliers as well as comments of users of the present system. Don't do anything with the data. Sit back, relax, and have a cup of coffee. Think about the comments and data. Try to form an impression of all of this—try to define a pattern. You might try to follow the guidelines we gave for automatic writing and write down thoughts that come to mind about the subject. For the parts-supplier example, some are listed below:

1. Present supplier doesn't carry enough supplies.
2. Supplier B doesn't seem to be well organized.
3. Supplier C seems cheapest.
4. Supplier A has the best quality and solution.

After you've done this, put it aside for a few minutes. Do something else. Return to it later and add to the list.

As you sift through your data, think of it in terms of the problem you defined in the first step. Doing this, you should be able to:

1. Evaluate data in terms of the problem.
2. Reduce the information to increase quantity and reduce redundancy.
3. Combine similar, related information.

There is often an urge to include important data that isn't directly relevant to the problem. You should cover that type of information by using a separate memorandum or appendix.

Writing the Report

You've collected the data and done your analysis. Now you need to sit down and write. Go through the steps we followed in chapter 5. We'll go through those steps in general here, and then follow up at the end of the chapter with some examples.

Objectives

Your goals in writing are to convey the particles of meaning you've gained from the analysis of the data. The particles need not have all the quantitative information in them. The particles can be supported by logical argument or by argument based on personal authority. As you'll see in the examples, the objectives vary with the type of report.

Strategy Decisions

Once you've decided to write a report, you must decide on the length. Arguing by personal image can shorten a report, compared with extensive argument based on logic and detached data. And sometimes it's wise to face the fact that long reports may not be read.

How will you organize your report? If it's to be a proposal, then the organization should be dynamic and persuasive. If it's a straightforward presentation of facts, then you might wish to arrange it by priority.

The direction is relatively easy to define. It begins with a statement of the problem and of the need for a solution. It ends with a recommendation for action, an overview, or a call for further research.

We spent a lot of time on how to define an audience. Now you must define your attitude toward the audience. Do you want to impersonally present data? Do you want to assume an advocacy position? Personal image follows from this. In most reports you want your audience to respect you as an expert in the situation. After all, you should know more about the situation than anyone else.

Outlining

We separate this strategy concern for special attention. Recall from the previous chapter that we have three basic types of outlines, shown in figures 6.1, 6.2, and 6.3. In writing a report, you usually follow the descriptive or the analytic outline. Consider the analytic outline here:

1. Introduction. Begin with a statement of the problem, and then state your qualifications and background in attacking the problem.

2. Situation. Provide description of the current situation and how it has evolved. The reader should know after reading this why the problem hasn't been solved, how the problem has grown, and how it became more severe.

3. Method. Present the methods used to attack and analyze the problem—the steps taken won't be in the same order as the methods employed. This section tells the reader about your approach. If you're using new methods, this section tells where they came from and why they're useful. Whatever the method, make sure the reader can understand the description of the method.

4. Analysis. Here's where you put the method and data together. Tables, graphs, and charts go here. When you're outlining this section, make sure the arguments flow smoothly in a logical sequence. This section can absorb 75 percent of the total length of the report.

5. Conclusion/recommendation. This section should bring out the major findings of the analysis and present an action plan for what to do next.

The outlining process for a descriptive report follows in a similar way using figure 6.1.

Tactical Decisions

The decision on evidence is related to the analysis you've done. The major question here is frequently one of format—table, chart, or other method. Allocating length to sections can be done at the section level for all sections except analysis; this must be allocated at a more detailed level.

Tone is an important decision in reports—perhaps unexpectedly. If you argue as an equal, you may fail because the reader thinks he knows as much about the subject as you do. A second, more likely possibility is to write as an expert who has done a thorough analysis of a situation. The use of jargon should be watched, although the potential reading audience of a report is usually better prepared for jargon than most other groups.

What's your attitude toward the situation? You should be

interested in something that has taken up this much time. But unless you're writing a proposal, you should also be detached. If your objectivity is doubtful, the effect of the whole report can be negated.

Putting It All Together

If you've collected all your data and properly analyzed it and if you've made all your decisions as we've outlined them—you virtually have the report written at this point. And since reports are generally valued for their timeliness and their information rather than for their literary merits, you'd do well to proceed with all due haste to a finished product.

Remember that most reports find their chief value as reference documents of one sort or another. That dictates that organization and accessibility are the most important aspects of good report writing. Use plentiful subheadings in your prose. Use lots of tables and charts where they're appropriate. Label everything carefully. Supply a good table of contents, even to a short document. If you're dealing with a long document, try to put together an index.[3]

But don't worry about writing deathless words. Remember that reports, although they're long, are generally less read than letters. If you find a report topic boring and useless, it may be just that. If you find it exciting, that excitement will find its own way into your writing.

Get it down. Get it organized. And get rid of it.

Project Status Report and Activity Report

Status reports and activity reports should generally follow the descriptive outline we presented in chapter 6. If you are the first to formulate such a report in your group, by all means try to adapt this outline to your needs. But frequently there's an established format for such reports—"the way we've always done it." There's no avoiding such formats. But if you find you must follow an established report format, there's no harm in following the descriptive outline in your abstract or précis. You might find that the report format is suddenly discovered to be cumbersome and confusing when your précis outline becomes part of the routine.

On deciding which evidence to use, remember that the audience may read a lot of reports over a fairly short time period. Make sure the data is significant—cost savings, efficiency, and so

---

3. *For the procedures in compiling an index, consult* A Manual of Style, *by the University of Chicago.*

forth. On allocating space to the topics, make sure that projects or topics of equal weight are given equal billing. The exception project—high visibility and high risk—can be reported separately.

Analytic Report

We mentioned a supplier example earlier. We posed a situation where you had to choose between three suppliers. Figure 7.6 shows the flexibility of the analytical outline. The first example is faulty because there's no presentation of the problem or the method.

Figure 7.6.   Sample outlines for the supplier example.

A. Improperly organized
  1. Present system
      a. supplier billing errors
      b. shortage of supplies
          i. typewriter ribbons
          ii. pencils
          iii. pens
      c. sales personnel
  2. Supplier A
      a. benefits
      b. procedures
  3. Suppliers B and C
  4. Recommendation

B. Better example
  1. Introduction
      a. statement of problem
      b. objectives and needs of study
      c. scope and sources

  2. Situation
      a. history
      b. problems
      c. benefits
      d. overall evaluation
  3. Alternative suppliers
      a. background of each
      b. benefits
      c. costs
      d. procedures
  4. Evaluation of suppliers
      a. range, type of products
      b. responsiveness, availability
      c. cost
      d. overall evaluation
  5. recommendations
      a. selection of supplier
      b. justification

The Corporate Gray Matter

Remember above all, when writing reports, that reports constitute the technical memory of your department—and of your company. They are used in legal matters, governmental investigations, policy decisions, and an almost endless array of other important situations.

The fact that you consider report writing to be tedious and redundant may be a product of your limited point of view. Governmental regulators are particularly demanding in the maintenance of regular reporting. You may find that your progress report on product development is used in any of the following ways:

1. an Affirmative Action suit
2. a patent infringement suit
3. a tax liability investigation
4. an internal personnel matter
5. constructing a budget
6. deciding on a price for your product
7. initiating or maintaining a line of credit
8. compliance with specific governmental reporting requirements
9. promoting you
10. new equipment acquisition studies
11. product trouble-shooting

There are very few facts which have only one potential use. And there are very few reports with only one potential use. Remember that you can always clean out your files and throw away old reports. It's not so easy to reconstruct times gone by and generate new reports on old material.

Exercises

In each of the following questions a situation is described along with an audience. Discuss whether a questionnaire is appropriate. Discuss what problems you might run into.

1. There have been some complaints about your new car model—Vixen. You wish to find out how serious the problem is.
   Audience—purchasers of the Vixen.
2. Your firm is coming up with a marketing concept for a new shampoo. You think it might be a good idea to test the concept before going into production.
   Audience—general public.
3. You are doing research to see what problems exist in using motion picture equipment.
   Audience—equipment dealers.

4. In problems 1-3 develop a brief questionnaire (5 questions). Discuss potential problems in conducting it. Have a friend or relative try it out. Compare their response with yours.

Write up a user manual/instructions on how to operate the following items:

5. Electric toaster.
6. Slide projector.
7. Paper clip.
8. Placement of a long-distance collect call.
9. Find a user manual for something you have recently purchased. Construct an outline from the manual. Evaluate the usability of the manual. What are some of the problems in using it?
10. A recent study developed the following data. You are to construct an outline to present the findings. What pieces of information are missing?
    a. Drug X is marketed in 28 states over the counter.
    b. 12% of the users of drug X have had headaches as side effects.
    c. Sales of the drug have been rising at the rate of 15% per year. Sales are now 2,000,000 bottles per year.
    d. Drug X has been shown to be less effective than drug Y.
11. Suppose someone is joining your group as a new employee. Develop an outline of a three-hour introduction to your department. Use whatever materials are available.
12. You are going to be presenting what you have seen for the last six months to a manager as part of a salary review. Develop a framework and outline for the presentation.
13. You are given the following tabular information. You have been requested to write a paragraph summary of the data for your management.

(in thousands)	1972	1973	1974	1975	1976	1977	1978
Sales— Product Alpha	32.5	16.7	15.2	14.8	15.1	16.2	16.3
Sales— Product Beta	2.4	2.8	3.1	5.7	8.5	22.1	20.3
Cost of goods sold— Alpha	22.5	18.7	16.4	15.2	14.1	12.3	11.7
Cost of goods sold— Beta	8.7	7.3	6.9	6.2	6.7	17.1	14.0

14. Find a report where the outline of what is being said is not clear. Discuss additional costs in time and problems that may arise.
15. You are to do a report on the four most profitable railroads (or whatever subject you wish to select). What sources are available in the library? Find three sources and take notes on each. Keep track of the time you are spending doing this.
16. Given a set of data on products over a five-year period such as that in problem 13, what are the benefits from using one of the computer-based methods discussed in this chapter?

Prepare an outline for a report for exercises 17 and 18 which is a combination of analytic and persuasive.

17. Results of a project comparing three types of office furniture and telephone systems.
18. Results of a study on acquiring a small firm specializing in solar energy cell production.
19. Take from your files your latest activity/status report. What purposes should it satisfy? Does it promote your work? Does it present problems with a perspective as to their importance? Does it repeat substantially from earlier reports?
20. Consider some recent reports you have read. What were the problematic and sustaining environments in the sense of our discussion earlier?

8
Committees: Gang Writing

Many of the most important documents in your business life will either be written by a committee or approved by a committee. Sad but true. You're probably familiar with the old saying about how a committee would construct an elephant: a giraffe's body with a long nose. Committees are inefficient, disorganized, diffuse, and frequently counterproductive. Why are they so prevalent in business? Because they have overriding strengths that make them useful. Unfortunately, most committees never use these strengths, because they have no structure in which to locate them. If you can locate them, a committee can provide the following services to your writing endeavors:

1. wide variety of types of knowledge
2. balanced viewpoints, with many opinions represented
3. wide variety of skills
4. good memory
5. thoroughness—as a result of the other four strengths

It's presumed in modern business that all committees use these strengths to the best advantage of their companies. It's common knowledge, however, that they don't.

In this chapter, we'll concentrate on two committee functions: generating an original document and approving a document submitted for consideration.

Generating an Original Document

Take seven efficient businessmen and set them down in a conference room. Be sure that each one is a good communicator. Ask them to write a document together—and watch nothing happen. They discuss the matter; they chew it up again and again. You've never seen a more thorough analysis—but you have to stand over them with a gun to make them get down to writing. Why?

Types of Committees

Principally, there are two types of committees, and neither is organized to produce anything:

1. The standing committee. Standing committees are ongoing, and they have specific areas of concern: budgets, product quality, employee morale, energy conservation, equal job opportunity issues. They usually have a formal structure, with a chairman who heads each meeting. They frequently publish agendas for their members, and they may conduct routine business fairly efficiently. But they have no mechanism for writing. They usually resort to asking one member for a draft of a necessary document—and wrangle over that draft until there's nothing left of it but hamburger. Thus, the standing committee document is passive (because it's full of compromises), nonspecific (because everybody has had a say-so on revision), diffuse (because the original viewpoint has been destroyed by discussion), and confusing (because there's no single author).

2. The ad hoc committee. Ad hoc committees are organized for specific one-time needs: new equipment needs, important promotions, specific marketing projects, employee benefits reviews. Although they may have formal structures, they have no established pecking order other than that dictated by the company's overall organization chart. They meander badly, dislike meeting, are under pressure to finish. If they have to generate documents, they are frequently interim documents—and they have the same problems standing committee documents have in regard to writing quality. Nobody has time to write; nobody knows what the consensus of the committee really is; nobody volunteers for work.

Both types of committees usually try to operate on some variation of standard parliamentary procedure. The chairman leads discussions, appoints people to do specific things, writes agendas. Certain members will be more vocal than others and will dominate discussions. When it comes time to vote, however, those vocal members will be buffaloed by the silent, nonrelenting members.

Since writing is viewed as a personal act, no one is willing to submit his writing to committee scrutiny until the committee reaches a point of desperation. Then someone will finally be appointed to write a draft—which will—as he expects—be torn to shreds when the draft is reviewed. Is that the only way to operate? In a word, no.

Objectives, Strategy, Tactics

In chapter 5, we listed a series of decisions to be made before pen is put to paper. They become overwhelmingly important in the committee environment. Because there are multiple minds at work—with multiple strengths and weaknesses—it's essential that all cards be laid on the table from the beginning. If there are irreconcilable differences in the objectives phase, then that's the place to iron them out, not later on, when a draft has been submitted.

Objectives

The first thing any committee has to do in writing a document is make up a list of the particles of meaning it intends to convey. Most of the heated discussion takes place during this session. Figure 8.1 illustrates the problem of getting a committee to agree on a single message. There are simply too many sets of particles of meaning to be easily dealt with. And what's required if you're to deal with them is a method.

Memory: The First Step   The largest problem with retrieving particles from a group is that they're stored in a number of different heads. So the first thing you need in your quest for consensus is a formal group memory. In a small committee, a note pad will serve the purpose. In a committee with more than three or four members, we recommend a chalkboard.

During the course of discussion, there'll be points brought up by the members that might lead to generally accepted particles of meaning. To keep them in the group's memory for future consideration, jot them down on your board (or pad). Be sure that what you jot down is a particle of meaning, not simply a piece of evidence, though. The table in figure 8.2 gives some examples of particles as distinguished from evidence. Remember that most particles can be noted in very few words, and that what we're after here are storage-level particles.

Figure 8.1.   Example of complex communications.

The Corporate Administrative Services Department has at long last been given the go-ahead to hire five new employees. There are six group heads: R. Smith (accounting); I. Ruskin (communications); J. Corrigan (systems); H. Hayman (purchasing); W. Wynne (planning); and L. Larsen (office services). I. Schank of personnel is to assist in deciding which groups get what positions. Each wants all five positions. There are six groups, so that a simple uniform allocation is impossible.

If a meeting is held and there's a lack of coordination, the result will be that no consistent division is made. Each person has an individual set of particles, which may support and yet contradict those of the other group managers.

Let's consider Howard Hayman in purchasing. He wants all five positions—two clerks, one purchase agent, one secretary, and one evaluation staff member. If he could get a new purchasing computer system he might be willing to give up the secretary position to Corrigan of systems. On the sentence level of particles he would say the secretarial position is clerical. He could then get support from Corrigan (systems) and Smith (accounting) since the evaluation staff member would support them.

Figure 8.2.   Particles of meaning as distinguished from evidence on the issue of instituting new equal opportunity incentives.

Particles of Meaning	Evidence
1. Minorities are underrepresented at present.	1. complaints from various social organizations 2. statistics on current employees
2. Recruiting methods for minorities are inadequate.	1. newspaper ads generate only WASP responses 2. college recruiters visit only large, tradition-oriented colleges
3. Companywide goals must be set.	1. government or judicial mandates 2. social mandates
4. Companywide goals must be met.	1. federal contracts unavailable until goals are met 2. corporate "good citizen" policy

Note that the particles listed in figure 8.2 are broadly representative of attitudes and policies. They aren't weighed down with data, aren't narrowed by case studies. Any objections that committee members have to these particles must be made on the basis of philosophy or principle—which brings us to the subject of compromise.

Compromise   Many of us were brought up to believe that "compromise is defeat on the installment plan." Whether that statement is true or not, the defeat of a committee can easily be effected by a refusal to compromise. The essence of satisfactory compromise is knowing when it's inevitable. Anyone who has arbitrated arguments or negotiations can verify that all-important rule. And the next major step in committee writing is to flush out the essential compromises—before any writing (or decision about writing) is undertaken.

If you've faithfully noted down all the major particles of meaning brought up by all committee members, you'll no doubt find that some of them conflict with each other. Look at the following list:

Particles of Meaning
1. Property tax relief is essential.
2. Government spending must be cut.
3. Essential services must be maintained.
4. No new taxes must be instituted.
5. Economic stimulus must be provided to business.
6. Schools must not be affected.
7. Employment must be kept high.
8. Renter relief must be included in property tax relief.

There are several areas of potential conflict. It's entirely possible, for instance, that numbers two and three of the list may appear mutually exclusive to the committee. The first step is to ask the committee members if any of them have irreconcilable differences with any listed particle. Take the particles one by one. Those that don't generate any nay votes can be allowed to survive for the moment. Obviously, then, some group discussion must be held on the particles for which there isn't immediate consensus. In the case of the list of particles, perhaps compromise can be reached by defining some of the following:

1. How much government spending must be cut?
2. Must that spending be across-the-board or could whole programs be cut?

3. What are "essential services"?
4. Can essential services be maintained by smaller budgets?
5. Can essential services be maintained satisfactorily at lower levels?

Obviously, there's no easy way around compromise. But issues must be met head-on at the beginning. There's no point in shelving such disagreements for later consideration; the only possible product of such a move is trouble at a later stage of writing the committee's document. So you negotiate and discuss, haggle and plead with each other until the group is ready to agree that there are no longer any irreconcilable differences concerning any of the stated particles (however they've been amended). It's important to exlude discussions of evidence at this point because: (a) it increases the areas of conflict; and (b) it may cloud the basic issues.

With a given amount of temper, smoke, and sweat, your committee, we may assume, will finally be able to compile a list of particles that's more or less satisfactory to all concerned. Then it's time to consider strategy.

Strategy

As you may recall, there are seven decisions and one task in the strategy segment of your preparations for writing. Some will be easily made; others may call for some discussion. They are:

format
length—general
method/organization
logic
direction
attitude to reader
personal impression
outline

The outline is the first task the committee will have to perform that relates directly to writing the document. And, in the best, most cooperative of committees, people will run for cover when it's time to outline. Nonetheless, there's a way to structure an outline discussion to produce results. Start off with a model outline for the type of paper you want to generate. Figures 6.1, 6.2, and 6.3 (see pp. 86–89) offer model, all-purpose outlines for three important types of documents: descriptive, analytical, and persuasive. You will find that most documents fit rather easily into one of these three categories. So submit the proper outline to the committee, and ask them to fill in the blanks. It's our experience that the outlining chore becomes considerably less odious when one of these outlines is used as a model.

Generally, if you have made the decisions we ask you to make before the outline is approached, the particles of meaning will fall almost automatically into their appointed slots. Remember that this outline will be a guide to the final document; it must be organized and worded so it is clear to every member of the committee—not just to the recording secretary. Once you have compiled an outline, we suggest a simple yea/nay vote to verify it. And from here on, the rest is cake. Even the writing chore will come relatively easily now.

Tactics

The five tactical decisions (evidence, specific length, tone, diction, and attitude toward topic) may be more time-consuming than some of the strategic decisions—simply because they must deal with specifics. You'll find that the more detailed these group decisions are, the easier will be the writing that comes at the end.

The only "killer" decision is the one we've called *evidence.* Despite the fact that the committee has now begun to pull together, there may be widely differing opinions on which evidence is the most potent, the least arguable. But this variation in opinions really represents a committee strength, rather than an organizational weakness.

A good committee is constituted of people from varying disciplines and responsibilities. A sample committee on equal opportunity incentives might include representatives from the following groups:

employee relations
governmental affairs
public affairs
manufacturing
financial management
administrative management

Each of these folks will have a distinct viewpoint and a distinct expertise in dealing with the issue. And, while they may be able to form a united front at outlining, they may tend to splinter over the issue of evidence.

The discussion of evidence must be shepherded carefully, and the committee must be persuaded to pick and choose among the many ideas. Why? Because if everyone's ideas were represented in the final document, the final document would be too long. It's as simple as that. A simple vote will suffice many times. You list all the potential data on a chalkboard, and vote on each piece of information separately. The ones with a consensus win. Be sure that you support steps 2, 3, and 4 in each outline. Numbers 1 and 5 need little (if any) evidence—whether you are dealing with descriptive, analytical, or persuasive documents.

One final hint on tactics: allocate space quite specifically. If you're dealing with a lengthy document, pin an arbitrary number of pages on each segment of the outline, and compromise from there. If the writing task is to be at all manageable, the members of the committee must agree on just how much space is to be devoted to each of the steps in writing.

Getting Down to It

If you've made all the decisions listed in chapter 5—made them together—you're ready to write. There are two approaches to this task: one for short documents, the other for longer ones. They are essentially the same process, though, a process of looking for a base document from which to work.

Short committee documents are likely to be sensitive. They frequently deal with subjects like personnel policies, legal matters, inquiries of various types. If they weren't matters of this nature, they wouldn't be relegated to the laborious committee process. And, since they're likely to be sensitive, it's practical to bring all the resources the committee has to bear on them.

Once all the tactical decisions have been made, the best approach to writing is for each member of the committee to tackle the job separately. The committee mandate must be followed by each member: each draft must be the author's response to the decisions made in concert with the other committee members. Each draft should follow the outline closely, and each draft should be required to use the same pieces of evidence. If these guidelines aren't followed, all the work on consensus so far has been wasted.

After all the members have completed a draft, they are asked to submit them *if they like* for the committee's consideration. Those who don't submit their drafts should hold on to them for use in the ensuing discussion. The drafts that are submitted should either be read aloud or distributed in photocopy to the members. A simple vote should be able to determine which draft will serve as a base document, a starting place.

From here on, the procedure is one of simple common sense. You prod the members for their revisions, suggestions, deletions from the base document. You prod them until there are no more changes, then you send the final product to someone for a final draft. Voilà! You'll find that, in most cases, the strongest draft will be the one chosen as base document. The most glib of the members will work with the words and style, and the "thinkers" will be able to do what they do best as well. No one will become destructive, because each member had to think through the subject as she wrote her own draft. The writing process becomes a simple logical extension of the decision-making process. You probably won't believe that as you read this, but you'll discover it in your own good time.

Getting a Document Approved

Despite all the foregoing, most committees will solve the problem of writing by delegation. One person is singled out to be responsible for generating a document for the committee's approval. If you've ever been the person looking for a committee's approval, you know how difficult that can be. Each committee member feels obliged to change something to leave his own personal imprint on it. Some members are implacable and relentless in their pursuit of the beleaguered writer. The whole can produce a document that has all the worst faults of a committee-generated document. In addition, the writer who submits the draft can be (or feel) insulted, degraded, unappreciated, and misused.

If you're selected to put together a document for committee approval, you must find a way to get some approvals from the membership before you begin to write. If you put together a draft that is subsequently revised again and again, the final document will be stale. Any document that is ground up and spit out over and over will lose its freshness, its coherence, its urgency. You must find a way to prevent that; if you don't, you'll find yourself with an unenviable reputation with the committee. You may be viewed as hostile, uncooperative, and opinionated as you try to reconcile the conflicting viewpoints of the members.

The way to avoid all this is to put together a planning document. Take all the decisions of chapter 5 and answer them as they relate to the subject you must write on. Answer them in writing and in order. Phrase your answers as clearly and as fully as you can, and submit that document to the committee for its approval. Let them wrangle with the ideas, rather than with your draft. Act as much the neutral as you can, but coerce them into approving as many of your prewriting decisions as you possibly can. Don't even consider writing a draft until you have approval of the particles and the outline.

If you can secure approval of the planning document, then approvals of the draft will be much easier to secure. The members will still quarrel with your language. Each member will still want to change something as a kind of personal signature. But there'll be no important organic changes—because you had all that approved before you put pen to paper.

When all is said and done, committees will still be committees. Some will remain quarrelsome and difficult no matter what you do. But with this technique, you've got a fighting chance.

Exercises

In problems 1 through 3, you're a member, but not chairman, of a committee. Using the methods in this chapter, discuss how you could convince the committee to be more productive.

1. An administrative committee advising the company president on computer system matters. There have been several meetings held—all poorly attended. The vice-presidents are now sending subordinates. You've attended as the representative of manufacturing. The meetings seem to deal with computer problems of a short-term, specific nature—of no general interest.

2. An ad hoc committee evaluating applicants for a management job in local government. Three meetings have been held dealing with all twelve applicants. But these have been general. There appears to be no specific plan.

3. A review committee for a companywide policies and procedures manual. The process seems okay, but the meetings are so boring that no one is attending.

There are a number of psychological methods for problem solving. Some of these are based on a committee process. One method is the delphi approach, in which members representing different viewpoints vote on issues. They are given averages, high and low scores of the group. They vote repeatedly until either a consensus or deadlock is achieved. It's similar to a jury system. For each of the situations in exercises 4 through 6, discuss whether the approach is appropriate.

4. A committee to raise funds from companies for intercurricular sports.

5. A committee assigned to study the feasibility of one of four integration plans before the city.

6. A committee to select artwork for the new gallery room.

7. It's sometimes said that committees are of little use and a waste of time. Using the example in figure 8.1 (page 123)

discuss what alternatives are available if the committee isn't formed.

8. One purpose of a committee is to share information. Assuming you've been named to be on a routine committee, what additional subjects might you like to cover through committee meetings? You represent marketing of the company's products—northwestern region. The committee deals with sales brochures. There are other regional sales people as well as a national sales representative.

In discussing particles of meaning we pointed out two types— sentence-level and storage-level. In each of the problems 9 through 13, identify both types of particles presented by opposing viewpoints in committees formed to deal with the subjects given.

9. Added money for school libraries.
10. Allocation of parking spaces.
11. Chamber of commerce committee on parade design.
12. Reelection committee for a United States senator.
13. Reduction in paperwork.
14. For each of exercises 9-13, assume a deadlock has occurred and discuss possible methods for resolving the deadlock.

9

Oral Communication: Interviews and Presentations

Up to this point, most of the material we've presented has been aimed primarily at improving written communications. Business is conducted largely on the basis of written communications, and they present the woolliest problems for most of us—for all the reasons we've discussed.

Perhaps the most crisis-ridden communication medium is, however, the oral presentation. Business has its fashions and fads, like any other field. Oral presentations are very much in fashion these days. It may be because writing skills are less dependable than they've been in the past. It may be because decision makers have less time to devote to reading. Or it may be that the limited feedback opportunity offered by writing is simply no longer satisfactory, given ever shorter lead times in important situations.

Whatever the reasons for oral presentations, they are here to stay. We're going to present, in this chapter, some applications of the communication principles we've established, intended to help out in oral communications of two principal types: oral presentations and interviews. We'll also do a brief survey of some types of visual aids commonly in use in management-level oral presentations.

Talking conveys information via the same communication path as writing, but with an extra wrinkle: immediate feedback. The path, as it applies to oral communication, is visualized in figure 9.1. The line labeled "feedback" indicates several distinct types of audience reaction to your message: their attentiveness, their involvement, their hostility or friendliness, their participation in a question-answer period. Feedback is continuous throughout the period of an oral presentation—whether or not you're aware of it. You must continually analyze it, adapt your information to it, reanalyze it, readapt, and so on. It's this process of constant analysis, adaptation, reanalysis, readaptation that makes for jitters. There's nothing wrong with jitters; the only way to avoid them is to die.

Figure 9.1. The communication path modified for feedback.

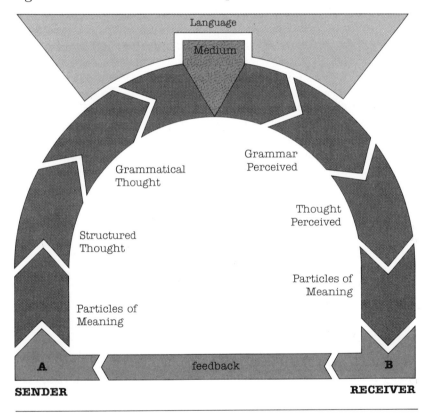

Throughout this chapter, keep in mind that you have an invaluable asset in oral presentation that is denied you in writing: presence. You're there as your message is being conveyed. You're there to clarify, to repeat, to reword, to supplement. And, to take full advantage of your situation, you must accept the jitters as part of the package. Know that you'll be nervous, and know that the nervousness will either pass or come under control. You probably won't faint. You probably won't begin to shake uncontrollably. And you probably won't make a fool of yourself either. Breathe deeply and slowly. Don't let your voice get squeaky and pinched. And remember that you've got the upper hand. The audience is there—hostile or friendly as they may be—to listen to you. You have work to do. Now that you've got yourself well in hand, let's talk about the forbidden subject once more: failure.

Why Does Failure Occur?

Failure can result from many problems. Some of these are:

1. misjudging the audience—such as giving a technical talk to a nontechnical audience
2. using too many visual aids or using the wrong ones for the room
3. allowing visual aids to dictate what you say
4. talking too long or too tersely—overexplaining or underexplaining your material
5. failing to interest the audience in the subject

And these are only a few. What can be done to help? This chapter contains some guidelines for preventing these problems. But first, let's narrow our focus. Let's consider the types of communications.

Types of Oral Communication

There are several types of oral communication.[1] Some of these are:

1. interviewing—information collecting
2. informal information presentation
3. formal presentation

Interviewing

An interview is a solicitation of information on a person-to-person basis. Another way to describe it is to say that it's a request for feedback. Data is collected through interviews to get information quickly and accurately.

There's a considerable amount of preparation for an interview—probably more preparation than actual interview. And that

---

1. *In addition, of course, to casual conversation, which is outside our bailiwick.*

preparation must be systematic and thorough. Basically, the preparation falls into two steps:

1. Develop any background materials you may need well in advance of the interview.
2. Prepare interview goals.

What are interview goals? Just what they seem to be. When you develop your interview goals, you must not only prepare the questions you'll ask, you must orient those questions toward certain types of crucial information.

You should approach your interviews with the following things in hand:

1. all the background information you'll need
2. an outline of needed information (interview goals)
3. an open mind
4. a tape recorder or note pad
5. a good memory

Interviews should be scheduled well in advance, to allow the subject to refamiliarize herself with the information she'll have to impart—and to assure that she'll have enough time and concentration to devote to the interview.

While conducting an interview (which should be done in person, by the way, and not over the telephone), follow the interview rules in figure 9.2 religiously. Use your good memory to record body language, reticence in committing to answers, approval or disapproval of questions, and cooperation. Above all, use your open mind to allow the interview to do its work. Don't use an interview to validate a personal theory. It will warp your questioning and limit the flow of information.

Figure 9.2. Suggestions for interviewing.

A. Before the interview
    1. Arrange for the length of time you need (asking for too much may delay the interview).
    2. Arrange for the interviews to be close to each other in time so as to minimize crosstalk between interviews.
    3. Set up a time that will be relatively free of interruptions.
    4. Avoid interviewing two or more people at once (with multiple interviewees, there may be too much extraneous data and dominance by one interviewee).

5. Ask in advance whether you may take notes.

B. During the interview
1. Be punctual—don't be late and don't overstay your time.
2. Be ready to construct questions on the spot to clarify the interviewee's remarks.
3. Listen to the tone in the interviewee's voice.
4. Observe body language and facial expression.
5. Don't wander off the subject. Get to the major points.
6. Don't bias the results of the interview with leading questions.
7. Don't rush forward with solutions.
8. Don't easily accept solutions put forward by interviewee, but show respect for their offered solutions.

C. After the Interview
1. Write up results of the interview as soon after the interview as possible.
2. Send to interviewee a note with results of the interview to avoid future misunderstandings—if possible, read it to him in advance.
3. Call after interview is conducted, thanking the interviewee for his time.

Now, let's consider a series of interviews. Each interview provides background information for the one that succeeds it. Consequently, the chronological sequence of the interviews takes on unexpected importance. You cannot possibly ask properly pertinent questions of data-processing supervisors (for instance), if you haven't already interviewed their customers for information on the quality and promptness of service provided. This sequencing of interviews is an important part of your interview game plan. Proper attention to scheduling interviews helps avoid:

1. interviews that are invalidated later through new information
2. repeat interviews covering the same ground
3. interviews that are incomplete in scope or depth of information

The last step in the interview process is to verify the information you've obtained. You do that in two ways:

1. Check it against other information.
2. Check your notes and memories with those of the interview

subjects. This can be done by memo in most cases: "My under-standing of last Thursday's discussion is as follows. . . . Please get back to me if you are not in agreement."

Presentations

Informal Presentations: Project Reports

You're in front of a small group presenting information on what you've been doing. Your talk might cover a collection of projects, a single project, or a whole department or division. Here's an example:

> Richard Donning is presenting a progress report to a group of managers. The project is a design for a new building. He starts talking about technical details of the glass and heat problems. The managers start shifting in their chairs. They don't want to hear about glass. They want to know if he's on schedule.

This leads you to the first step in planning your presentation—what does the audience want to hear about?

In a management presentation you're giving the status of the project. The basic questions for each project are:

1. Is it on schedule? Is it within budget?
2. If not, what's wrong?
3. What's being done to get back on schedule (or budget)?
4. What problems or solutions have developed?

These questions suggest how you organize your talk. Here are some guidelines for the sequence of your presentation:

1. Identify the project first—say what you're going to do and how you're going to do it.
2. Summarize previous status.
3. Give current status.
4. Present the actions you're currently taking.
5. Present unresolved problems and suggest possible actions (after reviewing problems from previous meetings).
6. Open the meeting to discussion.

There are several advantages to this approach. First, it relieves the audience of the anxiety of not knowing about a project. Second, it isn't boring because it moves at a rapid pace. The steps prior to discussion take fifteen minutes—at most. Third, it places emphasis both on problems and on your efforts to solve them.

What do you use for visual aids? You use the least you can get by with. If necessary, one or two charts showing status. We'll discuss this more later in the chapter.

Informal Presentations: Technical Reports

How about a technical presentation? You may be surprised, but it works in a similar way. Most audiences can only grasp the overall picture. They don't want a hundred equations in thirty minutes. They want to learn the essence of what's going on. Here are some guidelines for this type of presentation:

1. Begin with the technical problem you're going to deal with. Introduce it in nontechnical terms, and define its importance. Explain the organization of your talk.
2. Summarize what has been done in the past and why it fails to solve the problem.
3. Highlight your approach—data collection, analysis, validation, and so on.
4. Summarize your major findings. Give no proof or development. Instead, talk about what the findings mean in terms of an application.
5. Restate the problem and the impact of the solution.
6. Open the meeting to discussion.

Informal Presentations: Discussion Periods

The guidelines for both cases stopped at the point of answering questions. Many presentations unravel here. Speakers may respond in highly technical terms, or they won't directly respond to questions. Here are some suggestions on responding to questions:

1. Look at the audience at all times.
2. If there's a chance the whole audience cannot hear the question, repeat it.
3. Answer each question directly and briefly. Don't go into extra material unless it's pertinent.
4. If you don't know the answer, say you don't, and get back to them after the meeting. If a speaker lies, misleads, or deceives, the audience is likely to pick it up. In the long run, honesty is still the best policy.

Your Voice

Have you ever noticed that your voice is lower in pitch when you wake up in the morning than it is later on in the day? It's a natural phenomenon, caused by the fact that your vocal mechanism is—and has been for several hours—relaxed. And when your voice is relaxed, it isn't only lower, it projects better. You can reach an audience without yelling and without strain early in the morning, and you might not be able to in the afternoon. Here's an experiment you can try to prove it to yourself. Pick a favorite song, and take two showers tomorrow, one in the morning, the other in the evening. Sing the same song during both showers; odds are that the morning version will far outdo the evening one.

When you're relaxed, you're capable of better vocal delivery than when you're tense. The trick is to be able to relax your voice-producing system when the rest of you has the jitters. There are some things you can do that may help. The first is to yawn. When you yawn you stretch your throat, your chest, your larynx, and your soft palate. You also oxygenate your lungs more thoroughly than at any other time. A really deep series of yawns will do more to unjitter you and loosen up your voice than virtually any other exercise you can do. As any opera singer will verify, yawning is a most productive way to spend your time before going onstage.

Two general rules about your voice during oral presentations:

1. Your voice is most effective—and easiest to handle—when it's at its lowest pitch. It carries better. It forms words better. It strains less. If you notice that your voice is rising in pitch as you speak, it's only because you are tensing. It's a good indicator that you may be speaking too fast as well.
2. You can maintain your presence of mind and keep your knees from knocking together by breathing properly.

Your Breathing

If you take Americans, male or female, stand them up, and tell them to take a deep breath—they'll most likely do it wrong. They'll puff their chests up like bantam roosters and suck in their stomachs. That may be just the ticket in the army, but it's exactly the opposite of correct when you're speaking. To find out the correct way to breathe, you have to lie down. Lie flat on your back on a bed or the floor, and take a deep, relaxed breath. If you're relaxed, you stomach will seem to inflate like a balloon. Surprisingly, your chest will barely move. That kind of deep "stomach" breathing is the key to good public speaking.

Remember that the more oxygen you can get into your body, the more relaxed you'll be and the more alert you'll be. You can measure the difference with a balloon. Take a chest-puffing breath and blow it into a child's balloon. Tie it off. Now take a deep stomach breath and repeat the exercise with a second balloon. The difference will be obvious. If you breathe deeply, you'll be able to breathe more slowly. And you'll get more benefit from the breaths you take.

Since your vocal mechanism is highly interactive, you'll also find that your breathing will affect your voice production. Your voice will stay lower and more relaxed if you breathe deeply.

Your Enunciation

It goes without saying that if you don't pronounce your words clearly, your audience won't be able to understand you. Very few of us mumble so badly that we are totally incomprehensible, but when you're addressing a group of people, it's wise to exaggerate a bit. That doesn't mean try to sound like a British actor declaiming Shakespeare. It just means pay more attention to what you're saying:

1. Try not to fill in the silences in your speech with "uh" and "ah." These nonsense syllables are confusing to your audience—and they are also extremely annoying.
2. Try to pronounce all the sounds in words you use. When saying the word "little," for instance, be sure to pronounce the *t* sound in the middle. Don't convert the *t* to a *d*, and don't just make it a nonletter stop in the middle: "li-ul."
3. Remember that consonants don't carry. Vowels do carry. Try this experiment. Have someone stand across the room from you. Make a series of consonant sounds: *t, b,* and *k*. Then voice a series of vowels: *a* and *o*. The vowels will be understood much more easily than the consonants. As you read your speech in rehearsal, try accentuating the vowels at the expense of the consonants. You'll be pleasantly surprised at the result.

If you're breathing properly and have kept your voice at its lowest register, by the way, your enunciation will automatically be better.

Your Demeanor

Pick out one or two people in your audience and address your speech to them—not to the group. That doesn't mean you have to stare at those two, but you should speak to them. Speak as though you were carrying on a conversation with them. Remember that you have the benefit of body language, of gesture, of facial expression. You'd use those tools automatically if you were engaged in casual conversation. Yet somehow they disappear behind a podium. We're all afraid of making fools of ourselves. The interesting thing is, though, that the more you use your body (to a reasonable point, of course), and the more you employ a conversational manner with your audience, the less inclined you'll be to look the fool.

Remember that your audience will, more than likely, sympathize with you for a time at the beginning of your presentation. Unless they are extremely hostile, they'll give you a few minutes to work yourself into a demeanor that fits the occasion. If, for instance, you're presenting to a group of people who sit high above you on the company organization chart, you may be certain that you aren't the first nervous presenter they've seen.

And if you're breathing correctly, your manner will be easier and more fluid as a direct organic result. If you're breathing incorrectly—shallow, quick breaths—you may well be the quivering mess you're afraid of being. Your respiratory system is the only source of oxygen you have. And oxygen is the only means you have of making your body work smoothly and comfortably.

Writing a Speech

Isolating a list of particles of meaning to be conveyed in a speech is usually a fairly easy matter. Unlike written communication, oral presentations usually have easily stated purposes:

1. Defend the budget allocations we asked for.
2. Answer the audit queries.
3. Explain the new process we've developed.
4. Advocate one side of an issue.
5. Analyze market trends.

In business, oral presentations are usually given upon request, not initiated by the presenter. That means the oral presentation usually has questions to answer or tasks to fulfill. It's always easier to respond to questions than to make an initial statement. Unfortunately, it doesn't follow that it's easier to write an oral presentation than it is to write a letter.

When you write a letter, you're dealing with only one medium: the letter. You're writing something that will be read. You can use the tools of writing to convey your message: the wide vocabulary, the visual logic, the technical display ability. While there are difficulties involved, they're straightforward.

Writing a speech is different. You're doing something in two media at once: writing and talking. You're trapped between two sets of tools. You know that if you talk like you write, you may not make sense. And yet, you may not be able to write like you talk. It's a difficult task at best, and involves the development of a very good ear.

The best method of approaching a speech is quite simple:

1. Make all the decisions in objectives, strategy, and tactics.
2. Make an outline, using one of the sample outlines.
3. Start rehearsing and making notes.

What does such an approach do for you? First of all, it brings to the top of your conscious mind the answers to the decisions you need to make prior to any communication. It gives you a basis for composing your speech. It gives you a model outline, so that organization isn't a worry while you're on your feet. Most of all, it lets you deal with the medium you're interested in: talking.

This sounds so logical, but it's a procedure seldom followed. What usually happens is this: you're asked to do an oral presentation. You're worried or nervous about the prospect, and you salve your jittery nerves by writing out every word you plan to say. If you then follow the natural line of communication, you'll stand in front of your audience and read your comments verbatim—and bore them to death. You'll have built no room into your speech for modifications on account of feedback, and you'll lose all the benefits of presence.

If, on the other hand, you make yourself a bare-bones outline and practice extemporizing on that outline, you'll be committing the information you intend to convey to your memory in an oral framework. You'll be formulating what you need to say by saying it—not by writing it.

If you feel the need to have complete notes in front of you, try dictating your speech and having it transcribed. But whatever you do, resist the urge to read your speech. Your prime purpose in making your presentation an oral rather than a written one is to make it easy to respond to feedback. And if you simply read a prepared statement, you may well forfeit that advantage.

Visual Aids

In this age of advancing technology, there are some sophisticated crutches we can lean on in oral presentations. They're grouped under the generic name of visual aids. Depending on your resources, your company, and your lead time, you may be able to dress up your presentations with any of the hardware listed in

Figure 9.3. Visual and audiovisual aids.

Visual Aids	i. computer terminal
a. overhead projector with transparencies	j. computer terminal with graphics support
b. opaque projector with regular paper	Audio Aids
c. slide projector with slides	a. tape player
	b. phonograph
d. silent motion picture	
e. three-dimensional models	Audiovisual Aids
f. chalkboard	a. videotape cassette
g. magnetic board	b. 16mm film
h. chart	c. synchronized-sound slide or filmstrip show

figure 9.3. Examples of the highly sophisticated graphic CRT terminal are shown in figure 9.4; although these expensive and highly technical terminals aren't in common use today, they may be the wave of the future.

Figure 9.4. Examples of graphic CRT terminals.

This photograph was supplied by Intelligent Systems Corporation.

Figure 9.4. Examples of graphic CRT terminals.

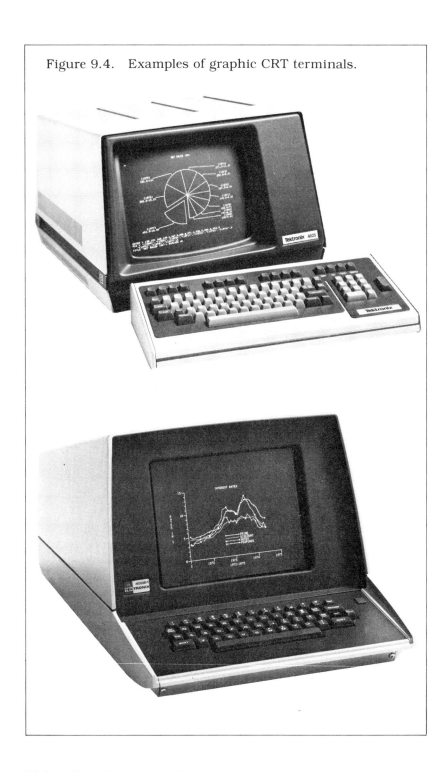

Visual aids can be a great help to the properly prepared oral presentation. They can also be the makings of a catastrophe. Since modern American businesspeople are inclined to look to technology to bail them out of difficult predicaments, the latter possibility is the more probable of the two. Why catastrophe? Because the trend has been to let the visuals dictate the content of the presentation. You have to make a speech or an oral presentation of some kind, so you have some slides made up. Then you fake a speech around the slides. In some cases, and with some experienced presenters, that may be an acceptable way of doing things. But in most cases, it courts disaster.

We're all familiar with what would happen if we began using crutches to walk. As we depended more and more on the crutches, we'd need them more and more. Finally we'd not be able to walk without them. It's the same with slides or viewgraphs or flipcharts. They are crutches; they should be used only when there's no way to explain a subject adequately without them. If you start using them as the basis for your presentations, your presentations will degenerate into support mechanisms for the slides.

Here's an easy rule to help avoid slide dependency: never order your slides until your speech is written or until you've been through your first rehearsal. By that time you'll know where you need slides either to pick up the slack in your speech or to explain a technical point. You'll be too far along to reshape your speech to accommodate a useless slide which came out looking particularly pretty.

Visual aids are a part of business life, nevertheless. A good and effective oral presenter must learn to cope with them and to make them work for him. But a good speaker will never let the visual aids become the master of the situation. Figure 9.5 lists some of the advantages and disadvantages of seven major types of visual aids.

Figure 9.5.   Advantages and disadvantages of some audio/visual aids.

Audiovisual aid	Advantages	Disadvantages
Overhead Gels	easy to use projector	copies may be a problem size of some projectors heat, noise of projector potential focus problems
Opaque Projections	simple to make and use visuals	same as overhead
Slides (lantern or 35mm)	projector is easy to use, often compact	time, expense to prepare slides noise of user not adaptive not all slide projectors take same size mounts

Audiovisual aid	Advantages	Disadvantages
16mm	inexpensive to duplicate change of pace for audience gives speaker a pause easy to transport film	expense and time needs operator minimal flexibility
Chalkboard	flexible, cheap simple to use allows extemporaneous talk	difficult in large rooms needs good lighting depends on good handwriting
Handout	saves audience from some note taking highlights major points	inflexible time-consuming preparation expensive for large audiences
Computer Terminal	shows dynamically what is going on demonstrates capability potential audience involvement	requires special facilities needs much preparation substantial risk of failure may be expensive

Remember also, when preparing visual aids, to keep them as simple as you can. Try never to crowd more material onto a slide or viewgraph gel than it will easily accommodate. Use color generously if it's available. Find and use a good reference book on audiovisual formats if you plan to use visual aids often. Figure 9.6 illustrates some commonly accepted alternatives in displaying technical or financial material on visual aids. Again, simplicity must be the key. Just like writing, oral presentations are based on an acquired skill. If you don't speak often, you probably won't

Figure 9.6.　Sample graphs.

a. Bar Chart—Vertical

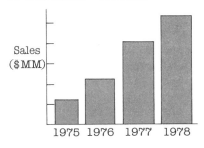

Sales ($MM)

1975 1976 1977 1978

b. Bar Chart—Horizontal

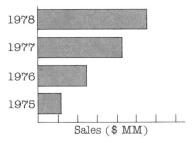

1978
1977
1976
1975

Sales ($ MM)

c. Component Bar Chart

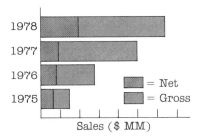

1978
1977
1976
1975

= Net
= Gross

Sales ($ MM)

d. Line Chart

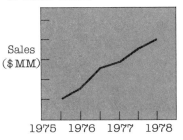

Sales ($MM)

1975　1976　1977　1978

e. Pie Chart

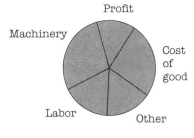

Profit

Machinery

Cost of good

Labor

Other

f. Exploded Pie Chart

Profits

g. Geographic Representation

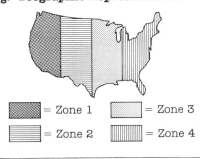

= Zone 1　　= Zone 3
= Zone 2　　= Zone 4

h. Pictogram

1974 Sales
$2.4 MM

1978 Sales
$5.8 MM

speak well. Since most of us don't have a chance to speak often, we must take full advantage of our bathroom mirrors—they are, after all, frequently our most critical audiences.

One Last Word

Keep your speech as simple and as brief as possible. Remember that jargon frequently doesn't work as well in speech as it does in writing. Acronyms can be especially confusing to an audience that doesn't encounter them often. Leave points that you think may be especially confusing to the later parts of your speech, placing them closer to the question and answer period at the end.

And rehearse. When you've rehearsed, rehearse again.

Exercises

In each of the situations in exercises 1 through 6, indicate the appropriate type of audiovisual aids.

1. A three-minute presentation to fifteen executives covering the progress in your department over the last six months.
2. A training session on office procedures to fifty new employees.
3. A technical presentation of a new mathematical method to do warehouse location.
4. An analysis of financial data for the finance committee at the bank.
5. Keeping track of personnel location during work hours.
6. Demonstrating how an oil refinery works.

In each of the exercises 7 through 12, data is given that is to be presented graphically. Select the most appropriate means of displaying the data.

7. Five-years' sales of three different products.
8. Allocation of city budget—this year versus last year.
9. Number of cars imported into the U.S. in 1974, 1975.
10. Location of underground water supplies in Oregon.
11. Growth in domestic sales as a percent of total sales for a five-year period.
12. The point in sales volume at which it's cost effective to build the new warehouse.
13. What we have talked about in this chapter applies to more formal presentations. We indicated that, although the number of presentations is limited, the need for practice still exists. Explore some of the following ways to get practice.
    a. Go to local meetings of city and school boards and agencies. Contribute in these meetings.

b. Join a volunteer group and indicate that you wish to work in the area of improving media communications.

14. An important capability we all need to have is that of taking tough questions that are posed spontaneously. You might think it's difficult to get practice in this, but it isn't. There are many helplines—for drug and alcohol problems as well as consumer problems. Some of these are sponsored by local radio or TV stations. Try volunteering a couple of hours a week in your time off work.

Give several examples in which presentations based on the audiovisual aids given in exercises 15 through 20 might fail.

15. Sixteen mm movie with sound.
16. Overhead projector.
17. Slide projector
18. Blackboard.
19. Handout.
20. Computer terminal.

MO:

_____

Part 4
Doing Your Part

10
Reading for Meaning

When you send a message, you're in control (at least in principle) from the time it's formed in the windmills of your mind until the time it's committed to a medium and sent away to the tender mercies of your reader or listener. You originate the message by retrieving particles of meaning from your mental files and organizing them into a coherent thought. You impose a grammatical structure on the thought, enabling it to "make sense" to a receiver. Finally, you commit it to a medium (writing, speaking) and hope for the best. And, while some part of this process may be a response to an outside stimulus (somebody asked to see your ideas on widgets), you remain the master of your words.

Receiving messages is a process that enjoys none of that advantage—although it's frequently treated as though it did. When you receive a message, you begin with a series of physical symbols of some sort (sounds, lines on paper, dots on a screen), and you must decode them until you see what the message is really about. It's easy to see why the responsibility for transferring meaning must rest with the sender of a message—but the receiver must be something more than a receptacle into which information is deposited.

Let's look at the communication path from the point of view of the receiver, and see what the steps are in receiving a message.

Attention—Or the Lack of It

There are two media through which we receive most of our messages: the spoken word and the written word. We also receive important messages through visual nonverbal communications (like body language), but the principal sources of storage-level particles are spoken and written words. Spoken or written messages can originate anywhere and can come to you via any number of different technical contraptions. The relatively efficient international postal and telephone systems have extended the possible communicators worldwide. It may be unlikely that you'll receive a telephone call from an old high school chum who now lives in Kuala Lumpur—but it isn't impossible. And with the multimillions of potential message senders out there, your chore as a potential receiver is fairly rugged.

Figure 10.1. Communication path (receiver's viewpoint).

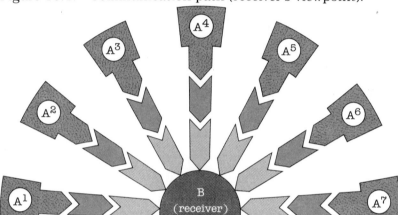

Each message in a different medium, from a different sender, on a different subject.

Imagine a situation in which you're standing alone in the middle of Yankee Stadium. Scattered about the stands are several hundred people, each of whom has a supply of baseballs. Any of those people may throw you a baseball at any time. You just have to stand there and catch them. It wouldn't be an easy task, considering that you have only two eyes (and you can't see behind yourself) and two hands. Yet your situation would be analogous to the task of receiving messages from the world of your acquaintances, business colleagues, clients, relatives, friends, and anyone else who cares to send one.

Your attention becomes a much-vied-for commodity in such a universe of possibilities, and it frequently fragments itself to the detriment of all. How many times have you listened all the way through a conversation without realizing that anything important was being said? How many times have you read a memo and missed the meaning (only to encounter the message-sender's "but I told you in that memo" after it was too late)? Many of us find ourselves concentrating more on the window or on our coffee or on last night's dinner than on the business at hand.

What's to be done about this fragmentation of attention? It frequently isn't possible to devote yourself to one message at a time. Not all of us are in a position to tell a secretary to hold all our calls every time someone drops by the office. Conversations are simply going to be interrupted from time to time. And reading is apt to be more often and more seriously interrupted than listening. There's not a whole lot that can be done about the situation, but awareness is the first part of a solution. Don't presume that just because you read through someone's document you understood it. You had two visitors, three phone calls, lunch, a fire drill, and a headache competing with that report. And odds are that not every storage-level particle managed to survive that barrage of enemy fire.

Awareness of the problem of attention and attention spans in today's highly interruptable world is the main component of a solution to these problems. If you're ready to admit that you rarely give a written message a fair chance the first time around, your problems are well on their way to being alleviated. Ah! But you say you always devote time to reading important letters, reports, and such things. You never let yourself be interrupted mid-message. Good for you (bravo, bravo), but that doesn't help as much as you might hope. Why? Because your attention has been ruined by the modern world, largely by television and radio. If you're anything like most people, you can't keep your mind trained exclusively on one thing for longer than a few minutes at a time. You want your music the length of a standard 45 rpm recording. You want your news in headlines like the all-news station on the radio (or worse yet, like television news). You like your drama and comedy interrupted every ten or fifteen minutes for a commercial (so you can stretch, talk, get a sandwich, go to the bathroom). You may read long books, but you don't read them straight through—only twenty minutes or so before you go to sleep. A short attention span does limit your ability to read lengthy documents or many documents one after another. And don't kid yourself about the issue of attention; it's very real. After all, the main reason people don't watch PBS (public television) is that it doesn't have commercials—and that is, as they say, food for thought.

Again, awareness is part of the solution, together with a pattern of reading tailored to your needs. Read in spurts if that's the way you read best. Don't try to wade through reports if you know your attention is going to wander. If it's unavoidable (say you have to read it before 3:00 P.M. for a meeting), then compensate consciously—take notes, underline passages, read aloud.

Your hands have a memory bank that is underused, and note taking is a way to get your hands to help you, the way they help you drive the car when you're not concentrating fully on the road.

Whatever you do, try to award each communication that comes your way the attention due it. Pay attention to yourself, too. See how your mind works—does it turn off automatically after four pages? Does it turn off at 10:00 A.M. until the coffee trickles down your thirsty throat? Then don't fight it: read four pages at a time, and quit for a while. Don't try to work through coffee breaks if you need coffee. You don't get things done quicker by struggling with yourself as well as with the task.

Once you've learned to deal effectively with your attention span, and have resolved faithfully to pay attention every time you receive a message, you're ready. Ready, that is, to deal with an even more annoying problem.

The Bugaboo of Surface Resistance

You may recall that in the first chapter we discussed two sentences in connection with the concept of grammatical thoughts:

1. Ordinary brown concepts stopped brilliantly behind six goatlike footballs.
2. Six brilliantly stopped brown behind ordinary footballs concepts goatlike.

Although neither sentence makes sense (at least neither was intended to), one is simply a string of words, while the other has the surface appearance of a sentence. The ordinary reader would read through the sentencelike sentence as though it made sense. That same reader would probably recognize immediately that there was no sense to be extracted from the second sentence. The difference between the two sentences is that one follows the rules of grammar and the other doesn't. One looks as though it ought to make sense; the other looks as though it couldn't possibly make sense. And therein lies the bugaboo.

Messages are fragile things. They attempt to move a thought from one mind to another by way of a string of less-than-dependable methods. Language and grammar almost always play an important role in that process; in most cases, there's no alternative.[1]

---

1. *Sometimes there is an alternative. An example is the case of extrasensory perception, if it does indeed happen as reported. It seems possible for a mind to receive an impression from another mind with no intermediary steps. Another example is the political phenomenon of charisma, by which a single person generates a kind of mob electricity that defies literal description.*

Language and grammar aren't mechanical tools, and different people use them in different ways. Consider the letter in figure 10.2. Would you consider it seriously? Many businesspeople wouldn't—largely because it encounters surface resistance on the part of the average business reader. It doesn't look like it makes sense (whether or not it actually does make sense). It might get a response but it would be a cursory one.

Figure 10.2.   Letter written with substandard grammar.

(Mr. Robert McGill, Vice-President, Consumer Affairs, General Automobiles)

Dear Mr. McGill:

A while ago—I bought a used sedan made from your Company. It don't run well and the seats are lumpy and the car costs a whole lot of bills to fixup to make it run again even though we have had the car three months. It is white with sunburn orange insides, and another problem is that it don't get good miles for the gas. The dealer Mr. Williams fixed the problems but it still don't run too good. We saved up a lot of dough for the car and we had to work at night and on weekends for some extra over time pay. Please write me soon and I am getting real mad.

Given the variation in people, living styles, environments, and educations, it's inevitable that people won't express themselves uniformly. That is, as they say, what makes a ball game. It also makes for some problems. Consider figure 10.3, for example. It's an extreme example of a stylistic peculiarity that quickly alienates the reader. Despite the importance (and the logic) of the message, the style frequently blocks clear reception. Why? In the first place, the message isn't written in normal English; it's written in a bizarre English dialect commonly called "legalese." It's a language known only to lawyers (and, if the truth be known, possibly not even to them) and clerks in law offices. Many people respond to such language with anger or with contempt—strong versions of surface resistance. If your response is something like, "How should I know what it means? I'm not a lawyer!" then you probably won't be able to decode the message. After all, how many people in the world would refer to payment by an insurance policy as "residue"? How many people would write a sentence that is eighty words long (as is the first sentence in figure 10.3)? And you, as a reader, react negatively to things like that. You reject the message because of the form it takes; you and the message are

Figure 10.3.   A message in the secret language of lawyers (taken from a life insurance policy).

"A person who is receiving under an option and who has the unrestricted right to withdraw the entire residue under the option or to whose estate any residue would otherwise be payable at such person's death may, unless otherwise provided in the election of the option for such person, designate (with the right to change the designation) a Contingent Payee or Contingent Payees to receive any residue payable at such person's death, the contingent interest of any other person notwithstanding.

"A person who has the right to designate a Contingent Payee for any residue may elect (with the right to change the election) an option for settlement of all or a part of such residue. Any designation, election, or change shall take effect only when Company files the request at the Home Office, at which time the contingent interest of any other person shall cease as of the date of the request, whether or not the person making the request is living when the request is filed."

the victims of surface resistance. You are the principal victim, however, because the message is of some interest to you (if the policy in question is your policy). The fault lies with the insurance company (for writing it) and the courts (for making it necessary), but the loss is yours because you don't (or won't) understand it. Figures 10.4 and 10.5 are more examples of this familiar problem.

Figure 10.4.   A message in noncommunicating jargon.

To: Accounting Department
From: Margaret Wiggins
Subject: Comments on Plant Design

This memo addresses the design of the new gas-processing complex. In place of the usual expander we are considering a radical type of centrifugal expander. Recovery work should be 3000–5200 rpm with operation at 7000–9500 rpm. There also appears to be no control mechanism for handling saturated water vapor in the gas fed to the low-temperature heat exchanger which can cause pressure drop due to emulsion formed by glycol and liquid hydrocarbons. Please inform us of the budget implications.

Figure 10.5. A memo in computerese.

To: Systems Staff
From: Allen Wright
Subject: OS JCL Job Changes

As you know our computer center is now running version 29.44
of release 19 of the operating system SMD. As part of the new
system SMD now logs I/O count, number to transfer units, record
size, terminal performance data, and job submission. Job cards
are now to be in the form
       //JOBJOB JOB 9991-1000, 'WU-47-JOHN DOE',

Individual Prejudices

There are some types of discrimination that no governmental or
societal force can mitigate. One of those is the personal reaction
you have to someone's writing style—and it can be the basis of
message failure more often than you might care to admit. Read
the three sentences below as an example:

1. John thought he'd already made the phone call; as it turned
out, he hadn't.
2. John relied on the mistaken assumption that he had already
contacted the client.
3. That idiot John forgot to call the damned customer.

Despite the obvious differences, the three sentences carry similar
meanings on at least one level. They might, as a matter of fact, be
three different person's comments on the same situation. They
evoke different responses in the reader. The first two are relatively
straightforward statements about John's forgetting the phone
call, although the second is somewhat more accusatory than the
first (one of the things good business people don't do is rely on
mistaken assumptions). The third is very strong and very slanted,
and if you are either John or a friend of John's, you might react to
it in the spirit in which it was written—bitterly.

    Now, suppose you hadn't read the first two sentences about
John's phone call. Despite the fact that you're John's best friend,
your only input is the third sentence. What will your reaction be,
short of checking with John? You might refuse to believe it. You
might presume that it's an exaggeration. You might presume that
the author of the statement is a hothead, or that he's covering up
his own mistakes, or that he's vindictive or panicky.

Without making any editorial comments about John, we can safely say that you—as John's friend—will refuse to store the message contained in the third sentence. You may check with someone if your interest is sufficiently piqued, but you won't store the information presented. That refusal seriously affects your role as reader; you're now deflecting information that was intended to get through to you. It's definitely the sender's fault that the message isn't getting through, because he took no care not to offend you—but again, the message failure may be your loss. You may take sides before you know anything; you may form an opinion of the writer that will color subsequent communications of more importance.

Are we suggesting that you simply become gullible and believe everything you hear? That you simply accept the statement "that idiot John forgot to call the damned customer?" Absolutely not. It would be true lunacy to believe everything you hear. But you should take care to *hear* everything you hear, to be aware that you're refusing certain pieces of information for specific reasons.

The Poorly Wrapped Package

Messages that arrive poorly put together frequently either aren't stored at all or are misunderstood. Two types of ill-executed messages deserve special attention: misemphasized messages and those that can only be adequately described as grammatical messes.

Problems in Emphasis

One of the most common errors in business writing and one of the most purposeful techniques in much advertising is the misplacement of emphasis in a message. Most rational people, when confronted with the question, "Do cigarettes really cause cancer and heart disease?" have no qualms about assenting. The tobacco industry still claims that nothing has been proved conclusively (which is a tribute more to their stubbornness than to their intellect), but the word is out nonetheless. And the word is printed on all cigarette packs and in all cigarette advertising. The people who write ads for cigarettes have managed, nevertheless, to shift the emphasis in cigarette ads away from sickness and death (the surgeon general's warning) to health, happiness, the great outdoors. It's an example of absolutely purposeful misplacement of emphasis. The complete message still contains the required warning, but it doesn't seem to make a whit of difference.

Change in emphasis can create problems even when it isn't so conscious and purposeful. And the victim may be the reader. Any reader who is victimized by a cigarette ad must want to be victimized, because the publicity on both sides of that issue has been strong. But the victim of a badly emphasized report or a badly emphasized letter has no one to turn to. So it behooves us, as readers, to examine emphasis in everything we read.

Look at the memorandum in figure 10.6. It contains one very important message to the reader. Can you tell what it is? It's not an easy task, because the message is well camouflaged. It hasn't been purposefully camouflaged, you understand, but the brush cover is no less thick because it's unintentional. There are two common reasons for this type of shift in emphasis:

1. The writer simply doesn't know which portions of the message will be of most interest to you.
2. The writer is writing off the top of his head and is simply more wordy on some subjects than others—or hasn't thought in the slightest about how his reader will understand what it is he has to say.

The second of the two is the more insidious—and far and away the more common. Most businesspeople write off the tops of their heads. And most businesspeople write without a hint of organization or outline. So it may happen that in a letter discussing two problems, problem A will get three paragraphs of complaint to problem B's one sentence. Then what will happen is that problem A will get all the attention and problem B will be ignored. The letter will get filed under problem A. And the reader may be victimized once again.

Figure 10.6.   A camouflaged message.

To: Payroll Staff
From: R. Wigle, Procedures Analyst
Subject: New Payroll System

As you are aware, we have been working on developing procedures for a new front end to our payroll system. The new part of the system will include a number of steps with which it is desirable to become familiar. Editing will be done directly on the forms. We have also seen increasingly substantial mailing and processing costs. Forms should be picked up in Linda's office for review. This will cut down mailing costs. Subsequent activities to the standardization of forms will include meetings with all staff members.

How does a person avoid the mistakes that seem inevitable with improperly placed emphasis—especially since the problem is widespread? One answer is defensive reading—analyzing everything you read for misplaced emphasis. The defensive reader runs the risk, however, of becoming a second-guesser, a person who disregards the written message entirely in favor of what he suspects might have been intended. That's all well and good for police psychologists, but it doesn't do well in the business world—people just don't like being second-guessed.

The real answer to problems of emphasis is the same answer that one might give to many reading problems: pay attention to what you read. Don't let yourself be led blindly around by the writer. Don't assume that the writer thinks something is insignificant because he only mentions it twice in an eight-page report. Read with a red pen in your hand and mark freely with it when you get to passages you'd like to remember later. Be aware that many people write with their brains in neutral—and that it's up to you to extract the meaning you need from the data that's presented to you.

Grammatical Messes

Not a lot needs to be said about messages that don't make good grammatical sense. They are ambiguous, confusing, and dangerous. Every corporation has people who are defined by their colleagues as "bright but can't express themselves." The stereotype of a brilliant scientist, for instance, is a lonely genius who speaks gobbledygook and needs an assistant to help him order a hamburger. It's an unusual but not impossible picture.

The important thing to bear in mind about grammatical messes is that they may have a message somewhere in them that you might want to know. Sometimes you can tell whether they say anything important; sometimes you cannot. An illiterate who sends your company a bomb threat that is badly worded gets the attention he deserves anyway. Your best client, who never had no schoolin' past the eighth grade, still gets your rapt attention and action when he requires it. But your colleague who never developed his writing skills may only get a smirk and a brush-off from you.

Generally, people who cannot communicate at all don't rise very fast in large corporations because they have trouble making themselves known. There are more exceptions to that statement than it seems possible, but it does function as a general rule. Consequently, many grammatical messes are directed at the businessperson from a position lower on the organization chart (a fact which tends to intensify disdain in some people).

The person who refuses to consider a grammatical mess simply because of the surface resistance it summons up in him is a foolish businessperson. Information—accurate and important information—isn't the proprietary property of the glib nor of the well-educated.

So What's to Be Done?

We've examined several of the most common bugaboos of reading—the various types of surface resistance and the ever shortening attention spans of the modern reader. But what can be done actively to improve reading comprehension and effectiveness? Two things are more important than all others: *consciousness* and *feedback*.

Consciousness

We said earlier that, while it isn't a good idea to believe everything you hear, it is a good idea to *hear* everything you hear. The same is true of reading.

The human mind has two basic modes of receiving information. One mode is limply passive; the other is an active learning and storing mode. The passive mode is usefully invoked by systems which play recordings to you while you sleep. As you dream, a voice drones on, "Comment vous appellez-vous? Je m'appelle Madame Orion." Eventually the theory has it that you'll begin to learn French while you sleep. Certain techniques aim for behavioral alterations while patients are asleep; the theory there indicates that nailbiters, smokers, compulsive eaters can be helped as they sleep. It seems to work for some people.

More commonly, however, this passive mode is the recipient of electronic images—those generated in a television tube. The eyes glaze over; the gaze becomes transfixed; and those little dots transmit themselves deep into our waiting brains. Have you ever found yourself staring at a television program that really didn't interest you—and you couldn't quite figure out what you were doing watching it? Most of us would answer yes if the same question were put to us concerning commercials. Of course you sit there and watch them; otherwise how could you recognize the jingles? Since the average American adult watches television at least three hours a day, that mode of receiving information is a commonly used one. You learn tons of trivia abut medicine from the doctor shows. You learn some legal loopholes from the cops 'n' robbers and lawyer shows. You learn all sorts of things from the quiz shows. And you learn more than anyone has a right to know about dog food from commercials.

Nevertheless, the semiconscious input that television represents isn't very dependable. Have you ever tried to remember what was actually said in a quiz show? You can't remember the questions, much less the answers that you thought you'd wow the folks at the water cooler with. Many people can't even remember what happened on their favorite dramatic shows last night (come on, admit it, nobody's looking). And there's a good reason for that disturbing phenomenon. The information you receive—and store—from television input is not kept in any particular order in your memory banks. In other words, your memory of the quiz show may be stored in a cluster of facts like:

fat lady from Iowa
toothpaste commercial
Norman Conquest in 1066
emcee's tuxedo with velvet collar
sandwich and coffee
money—why not me?

In order to retrieve the information about the Norman Conquest, you'd have to rattle the information about the fat lady, the toothpaste, the tuxedo, and so forth. Why? Because that's the way memory works—you retrieve memories by finding out where they're stored in your brain. And when the Norman Conquest is stored next to a fat lady and a sandwich, you may never find it.

On the other hand, if you'd learned about the Norman Conquest from a textbook, your cluster of nearby facts might look something like:

William the Conqueror
Battle of Hastings
King Harold
Norman Conquest in 1066
Edward the Confessor
Bayeux Tapestry

Why the difference? Because when you read for meaning—that is, when you read consciously—you make an attempt to store material in an easily retrievable niche in your brain. You store it in an organized manner near other related information. Then, when a mention is made of William the Conqueror, it summons up some of the other information nearby.

It's possible for the human brain to seem to operate smoothly when, in fact, it's sputtering and choking. Just that your eyes move along a line of words, you know all the words, and you read them all to yourself doesn't mean you've read the message contained in those words. And it certainly doesn't mean you've stored the message for future retrieval. It's even possible to read something with your attention focused on it (like watching television) and still not get the message. It just doesn't soak in, or it soaks in in strange, unlocatable places. All of us end up with some memory clusters like the following:

the beach and the sand
blue skies
cool water
meeting with Harold on Friday
beer
volleyball

It pretty much goes without saying that you're not going to remember the meeting with Harold on Friday.

A Word About Files

Machines and technology are extensions of our bodies. A carpenter's hammer is an extension of his hand—it allows him to do things with his hand that he could not do without the hammer (pound nails). An airplane is an extension of our feet, allowing us quick and comfortable transportation between distant points. The theory behind technology is that it improves things:

Unaided Body Function	Machine	New Ability
walking	airplane	NYC to LA in five hours
talking	telephone	long distance talking
remembering	files	lose paperwork faster

Losing paperwork faster obviously isn't the purpose of files; they're intended to serve as an expanded, more exact memory. But they often don't work that way. Why is it that some things don't work well? Simple things like files just don't receive any priority or attention in day-to-day life. How many businesspeople have no idea whatsoever of how to find something in the files? How many businesspeople have no system whatsoever in filing? How many businesspeople only file things when they're finished, because otherwise they'd never get done?

File cabinets are an extension of your head; they're supposed to be a well-ordered memory bank that increases the ability you were born with to remember things. Properly ordered files can answer a question with amazing rapidity:

How many kegs of beer did you buy for the party?
On what date did you receive a memo from Janet?
When will your FICA deductions stop this year?
Was the order from ABZ filled from stock or back ordered?

All these questions can be answered quickly and easily by locating the proper piece of paper in the files. Your files provide a service that your memory can't begin to match. With that in mind, why is it that most businesspeople don't know (don't care?) how their files are organized? It's a well-known problem, and file jokes are common around most offices ("Where's the report? Probably under *l* for 'late' or *c* for 'crazy' "). Nothing ever is done; file reorganization gets the same treatment year after year—put it off until later.

The thing to remember about files is that if they're a mess, then you're a mess. If you suspect your secretary of being scatter-brained about his filing, remember that the files are part of your head, and it might be a good idea to know what's going on in there.

Feedback—Completing the Path

Very few communications are entirely one-way. Most solicit some type of action or response, regardless of whether that action or response is actually generated in the reader or listener.

There is a specific type of response that deserves mention in this chapter on reading: feedback. Feedback is the response made to a flow of information. Sometimes there's a direct request for it:

"Do you understand what I said?"
"Are there any questions?"
"I hope I made myself clear."
"Perhaps my explanation was too technical. . . ."

In such cases, you would normally respond either by affirming that you received the information and have no questions or by querying further if you aren't entirely satisfied. But what of the times when feedback isn't requested? Don't you still have occasional questions?

Remember that it's the sender's responsibility to see that the message is transferred intact from his head to the head of the receiver. Just so. But remember also that, in many cases, it's the receiver who's the loser in a case where an important message fails:

"Watch out for that car!"

The unfortunate fact is that many message senders in this advanced world of ours aren't aware of their responsibilities in sending messages of importance, and receivers are frequently in the dark about what's being said. That's where we hit the responsibility of the listener or reader. It's the receiver's responsibility to speak up when he has not understood what's being said. Further than that, it's a good idea (though not mandatory) for receivers of messages to consider sending verifying messages back to senders after receiving complex or extraordinarily important messages of absolute clarity:

Dear Sam:

Got your note of 10 June about interest payments to clients. We fully understand what you are suggesting.

Regards, Jim.

It's like verifying an order received by a sales department. If someone sends you an important message, it's a good idea to let them know you received it.

If the world just operated that way all the time, things would be better. But even if you don't receive the feedback you'd like from people you send messages to—there's no reason why you can't be a responsible listener and reader for the rest of the world, is there? Remember: do unto others . . .

Exercises

1. Select five pieces of writing for review. If possible, choose pieces you haven't read before. Read each and determine whether you're having a difficult time because of surface resistance.

What's wrong with the sentences in exercises 2 through 4?

2. If such a collection threatens little future challenge to the Louvre or the Metropolitan, for rank among the greatest art museums in the world, it seems sure to become the greatest, anyway, that money can buy, once a small legal complication over its endowment is dispensed with by the courts.

3. It was agreed that the scope of this objective has been

broadened to include formal documentation of our project selection procedures, which includes A&D.

4. Although several preliminary steps have been taken review possible configurations and cost, we decided not to pursue further for now because of the perceived coordination problems for us as well as the current lack of interest by the computer centers.

5. There are several problems that relate to emphasis in the wrong place. One problem is that of camouflage. The news or data presented is related to the main issue, but the connection hasn't been made by the writer. You're then forced to make the connection and continue to connect the issues as you read the article or memo. A prime example occurs in the newspapers, where background reports on topics are mingled with issues of the day. Select two of these and practice relating it to a central issue.

6. What we've discussed is how to read more effectively. A related situation is how to tell someone that their writing is difficult to wade through. First you must verify this with other people. If the writing is a problem to read for several people, you might try one of these methods:

   a. Respond to memos or requests based on a logical but incorrect reading of the request.

   b. Don't respond at all and wait for the writer to see you in person or to write again.

7. Not only do you need to read more effectively, but you also need to be more selective in your reading. Over the next week, divide your mail each day into three piles—those to be read now, those to read sometime soon, those to be scanned or pitched in the trash. You should find that you can easily survive by reading the material in the first pile.

11
Evaluating Yourself as a Communicator

erhaps the most troublesome part of communicating is that you seldom know whether you've done it. When you're successful, people merely absorb your information and proceed to the next step. When you aren't successful, they still absorb something (even if it's wrong or incomplete), and they still go on to the next step. Life doesn't halt because a message has failed; it can be a lot simpler and easier when messages get through as intended—but it seldom collapses when they don't.

Because everything doesn't collapse (or even visibly falter, sometimes), finding out whether or not a communication was successful can be quite a chore. Look at the memorandum in figure 11.1, for example. It intends to convey a body of information—and seems to do an acceptable job, from all indications.

Figure 11.1.   Memo with no request for feedback.

To: Distribution
From: Ronald Alwy
Subject: Edwin Hill's Background

Edwin Hill received his B.A. degree in business administration at the state university in 1971. His major was accounting. The courses he took included introductory accounting, intermediate accounting, cost accounting, advanced accounting, marketing, finance, auditing, and tax accounting, as well as courses in computing and behavioral science. He became a member of several honorary societies, including Gamma Rho Sigma. After graduation he worked for an intermediate-size accounting firm.

He worked in this position for two years. He worked on cases in both auditing and tax. He is married and has two children—a boy 8 years old and a girl 5 years old. He returned to school in 1973 and received his MBA degree in 1975. He is currently working at the firm of Householder and Wickes. He is pleasant and easygoing. He is highly motivated. He should do well in his chosen career path.

But what indication will the author have that the information has been received completely and accurately? Probably none. Fred will read the memo, file it away for reference, and the matter won't come up again. Ron will have no positive feedback to let him know that everything went all right.

Feedback

Because we seldom encounter verifying feedback on the success or failure of our messages, we usually go on the precept that if nothing jumps up and bites us, things are okay. If Jim Connaught over in purchasing doesn't query my request for a staple gun—then I'll probably get the staple gun without hang-ups. In that sense, as the old saying goes, "No news is good news." That is, until a similar (but wrong) order arrives—and you're left waiting for the staple gun you need.

In the case of the staple gun, it's usually easy to figure out what went wrong. You didn't have enough information to pass along, or the stock number was wrong, or the model you wanted isn't manufactured any longer. It's not always that easy, however, to troubleshoot communication breakdowns. The best you can do is keep your antennae open to trends in the way the world responds to your messages, and to look analytically at the breakdowns that do occur visibly. The clues you have to work with in the detective game of "how well do I communicate?" are all in the area of feedback. And feedback is a changeable thing. Basically it comes in three guises: positive, negative, and nothing.

Positive feedback is easy to accept; it's reinforcing, encouraging, pat-on-the-back stuff. Negative feedback is less pleasant. It's commonly encountered as "I just don't understand what you're saying," or "I didn't see that in your letter," or "I don't recall reading your letter." Nonetheless, while it may make the hair on your neck bristle, it's the most valuable kind of feedback you can encounter because it's as unmistakable as a brick wall.

The most difficult variety of feedback to deal with is the kind we've called nothing feedback. You send a memo to someone and you get no reply at all. You order a magazine and it doesn't come.

You make a phone call to someone who's away from his desk and he doesn't call back. You leave a deposit in the night slot at the bank and you never get a receipt in the mail. It's difficult to isolate what went wrong with nothing feedback, but it's certain there was a short circuit somewhere. You have to view it as overall negative unless something shows up to disprove that analysis.

What we'll be doing in this chapter is traveling down the communication path looking for the pitfalls, the banana peels, the custard pies along the way. And, in so doing, we'll hope to develop a method of self-analysis that will help you improve your ability to communicate. Large order, that.

Recognizing Feedback

To work with feedback, you've got to know how to identify it. Feedback is the response made to a flow of information, but that definition will have to be amplified a bit to make it more useful. We've already identified three types of feedback, so let's see if we can find it hiding in a couple of examples.

Pitfalls, Land Mines, and Other Sneaky Traps

Gird yourself. Put on your armor, grab your sword, and jump on your charger. We're going to travel down that most dangerous of roads—the communication path. There'll be dragons aplenty; some of them will pop out and roar at you; some of them will lurk in the bushes. But we'll find them all, never you fear.

There are seven major locations on the communication path, and we're going to explore the types of things that can go wrong at each of them. You may recognize symptoms of your own experience in some of them; very few of us have managed to avoid all these pitfalls over the period of our business lives.

Incorrect Retrieval

The first stop on the path is labeled particles of meaning, and here you find an important potential failure in transferring a message from one mind to another—incorrect retrieval of particles of meaning from your memory banks. If that sounds overly technical, you may recognize the problem from one of these examples:

Example A
You're walking along the street with a friend and you spot a fellow you used to work with. You approach the ex-colleague, and the dialogue goes like this:
You. How are you? It's good to see you!
He. Fine, thanks, John. Still at the same place?

You. Where else? Hey, I'd like you to meet a friend. Frank Spellman, say hello to Artie West.

He. My name's not Frank Spellman; it's Hank Spielberg.

You. Oh.

That may seem like a minor occurrence (although it never seems so at the time), but suppose it were transferred to the following:

Example B
You've written a report suggesting a restructuring of the graphic services department in your company. That's the group that makes up all the slides you use in sales presentations, and its staff members report to the marketing vice-president. Your suggestion is based on a series of encounters you had with graphic services last week. Nonetheless, your report misnames the group, and you simply term them the "art department." Your report doesn't name any names; it simply states that systems in the art department are cumbersome and repetitive. Turns out, of course, that there really is a group called the art department, and those people report to public relations. Your report is routed to the public relations vice-president, who responds to you that she was unaware that marketing personnel were trying to give her people work—they already have enough of their own.

Both examples are basically just mistakes in retrieval. You thought the fellow's name was Spellman when it was Spielberg. You thought the graphic services group was called the art department.

The same process accounts for foul-ups that are a great deal more serious—with no appreciable difference in the process. Suppose, for instance, you recall incorrectly that vendor A has sold you a defective product, although it was actually vendor B. You write a harsh letter to vendor A, who writes back to your superior telling him you've got a screw loose somewhere. Mistaken retrieval.

Mistaken retrieval can also be incomplete retrieval. You recall that you cashed a check for twenty-five dollars this morning, but you forget that you spent twenty dollars of it at lunch. You stop off for a drink on the way home and, faced with a six-dollar tab, you find that you have only five dollars.

If you find you're trapped in situations like these with any frequency, you need to pay attention to the very first stop on the communication path. Labeling such mistakes as careless or absent-minded does nothing to improve for the future—even though such labels may appear to be accurate. What can you do? The situation is a little like trying to stop smoking. Very few people are careless on purpose; very few would-be nonsmokers light up with glee. It isn't a habit that's easy to break. What you have to do is make the customary resolutions to do better—and set up some fail-safe devices to police yourself.

First, admit to yourself that your memory isn't what you'd like it to be, and begin depending on your files a bit more. That may mean a hitch on file cleanup detail, but if it does, so be it. One of the original uses of secretaries (before they became clerk-typists) was retrieving and checking data. A good secretary probably knows as much (or more) about the files as you do and may be a good clearinghouse for accuracy of written material. If you don't have a secretary or a willing colleague, you have a more difficult time ahead. You have to set yourself traps—whatever it takes to remind you to mistrust your memory.

Admittedly, there's little more to be done for faulty retrieval of data than to check it more fully. Since the process takes place in your head (or in your head's office extension, the files), it's difficult to control if you don't do it yourself. With the other loci on the path, there are more concrete things you can do.

Structured (and Not-So-Structured) Thoughts

After you've retrieved your data and verified it, you begin to structure a thought to be communicated. Now your message begins to take the shape it will have when it's sent. You're now moving from the objectives segment of your battle to the strategy decisions.

Problems at this stop on the path may take several forms. One of the most common is simple confusion on the part of your reader or listener. The following two examples illustrate the type of feedback you might get from this confusion:

Example A
You're in the marketing department of a consumer-products manufacturing company. This year, your company has volunteered to spearhead the fund-raising drive for a local charity, and you've been asked to help in the solicitations. You write a letter to several of your clients and colleagues, mentioning the following points:

1. Community Chest is a worthwhile charity and a very active one as well.

2. Your company stands behind the current year's drive and is offering a matching-gift program as a community incentive.
3. Gifts and pledges should be sent to the Community Chest at a local address—and your company's matching-grant fund should be mentioned specifically.

Things go well for the most part, but for some reason the pledges and checks are all sent to you, instead of to the Community Chest. At first you wonder what foolishness prompts such action, but then you are inundated by a flood of letters and checks, and it becomes apparent that you did something wrong.

Example B
You become aware, through the company grapevine, that a position is open in a department you're interested in. You decide to write a letter to the manager of that department (who is not an acquaintance of yours), detailing your qualifications. You write the letter on plain paper and mail it from your home, because you're not particularly anxious for your current manager to know you're looking elsewhere, even in the same company. You find out that another person has been hired soon after, and you receive a letter in the mail—at home—telling you that it is the company's policy to hire from within whenever possible. You have been excluded from consideration because the letter you sent didn't emphasize (apparently) the fact that you're already an employee of the company.

The problem in both example situations is that you can take a group of particles and string them together in any number of different ways. Each of those patterns has a slightly different emphasis and thrust from all the others. Why? Because communication must take place within the dimension of *time*.

Time (the First Shall Be Last . . .)

Anyone who has watched "Star Trek" or read H. G. Wells's *The Time Machine* knows that there's a fourth dimension: time. In science fiction, people manage to skip through "time warps" to find themselves living hundreds of years in the past or in the future. And, while time warps may be fictional, the fact of time as a dimension in our lives is not.

The practical impact of time on written communications is that every message must have (like every good piece of fiction) a beginning, a middle, and an end.[1] And the arrangement of pieces of a message in time strongly affects the shape and emphasis of the message as a whole. Look at the example in figure 11.2. The particles that compose the message are arranged in three different ways—to three totally different effects. Nothing has been changed but the order (and the sense).

Figure 11.2.   Three versions of one message.

Particles of meaning to be transferred:
1.   Allan Reynolds is the manager of purchasing.
2.   Allan has just resigned—suddenly.
3.   Our purchase order is still hung up in purchasing.
4.   The new manager of purchasing is William Jones.
5.   Meet with Jones to expedite the purchase order.

Dear Richard:

Allan Reynolds has just resigned as manager of purchasing at Alpha Corporation. We have a pending purchase order with Alpha. If Allan was your contact there, I suggest that you immediately contact his replacement, William Jones, to expedite the purchase order.

Dear Richard:

I have been reviewing the status of our pending accounts and contracts. For your area there are four purchase orders pending. One is with Alpha Corporation, located in Bayview. By the way, I have heard that Allan Reynolds, manager of purchasing at Alpha, has resigned. I understand also that Allan left quite suddenly. Also, I have learned that his replacement, William Jones, is on board. I have no further information. You should continue your efforts to finalize the purchase orders outstanding by the end of the year closing of the books.

Dear Richard:

I have just received word that William Jones is the new manager of purchasing at Alpha Corporation. Mr. Jones replaces Mr. Allan

---

1.   There are, of course, methods of communicating that are relatively free from this time constraint. The reason that a picture is said to be worth a thousand words is that pictures communicate immediately—no segment of a picture is first or last unless it's simply too large to be seen at a single viewing.

Reynolds. By the way you have a number of outstanding purchase orders. One of these coincidentally is with Alpha Corporation. The controller has informed me that you should try and get all oustanding purchase orders filled by the end of the year close of business.

Many confusions result from this phenomenon. Despite best intentions, placement in a message dictates emphasis to a very large extent. The fact that you gave an address for the Community Chest office in example A didn't stop people from sending checks directly to you. Why? Because your instructions were near the end of a two-page letter—and nobody reads all the way through a two-page charity appeal; they're either going to give or they aren't. So they sent the checks to the return address on the envelope or the letterhead.

How do you avoid this kind of confusion? In the Community Chest example, it's easy—you enclose a return envelope with the correct address. You don't want to shift the emphasis in the letter, because you're concentrating on soliciting a donation, not on giving instructions. In the case of the job applied for and lost (example B), the problem is more complex. The resume you enclosed in the letter showed your current employment at your company—and by rights the manager should have noticed that (see how easy it is to blame the receiver for missing the message?). But he didn't, because you deliberately misled him, and because very few people look at resumes at all unless you coerce them. Your letter had the appearance of a letter from the outside, so it was treated as a letter from the outside. Is it a no-win situation? No way. The easy solution is to enclose your card, or use the company's letterhead, even if you want to mail the letter in a plain envelope from home. Better yet, call the manager and ask him if you may send a resume. It would be awkward for him to refuse you, and then he'll be expecting your letter, which means it'll have a much better chance of getting read anyway.

Length (. . . and the Last First)

The fact that time and placement can and do warp messages leads us into the most common of all errors in business writing. To say that much business writing is too long is a commonplace; everybody knows that there is simply too much to a lot of what we read. People don't seem to know how to say what they want to say and then shut up. At least that's the way it seems when we're receiving; it may be totally different when we're on the sending end.

Some experts are inclined to put arbitrary limits on the length of letters and memos: "Never write a letter longer than two pages." That sort of rule is hogwash because it's useless. The letters that must exceed two pages are important and they frequently can't be shorter. And, besides, we've read a lot of one-page letters that were one page too long, and the rule wouldn't help them anyway.

How do you tell if a letter is too long? With a letter that you've written, it's frequently hard to tell because you're too close to it. But there is a way to tell if you're consistently writing too much. If people seem to miss what you say in the body of the letters you write, you're writing too much. If you find that the requests you put in the next-to-last paragraph never get noticed, you're writing too much. And if you find that you have to reread a letter while you're writing it—just to see exactly what you've said—you're writing too much.

Most letters should be an explanation of a single thought. A very few particles of meaning should totally dominate the entire missive. And if you have a small number of particles of meaning, you should have a small amount of writing. Somehow people, seem to think that if you say something five or six times in five or six different ways, you have a better chance of communicating. Judge for yourself which memo in figure 11.3 is more effective.

Figure 11.3.   Variations in emphasis.

To: Corporate Staff
From: Algeline Metcalfe
Subject: Personnel Meeting

All exempt category staff members are requested to meet with the marketing manager at 8:00 A.M., on Wednesday, April 18. The location of the meeting is 4335. The meeting will last until 11:30 A.M.

To: Corporate Staff
From: Algeline Metcalfe
Subject: Personnel Meeting

This is to notify you of a marketing meeting at 8:00 A.M., on Wednesday, April 18. This meeting notice applies to all exempt employees in the corporate staff. It includes grades 14-24. The meeting will be held in room 4335 of the corporate building. If you are unable to attend the meeting, you should let the secretary of your manager know by 4:15 P.M., on Monday, April 16.

For grades 14-19, you should notify your supervisor if you cannot attend. If you notify the secretary or your supervisor, then you should also arrange for a make-up meeting to discuss the subjects covered at the main meeting. If there are problems with the make-up meeting then you should notify me immediately. The meeting will last approximately 2½ hours.

A general rule for length is to say what you have to say as briefly as you can say it and then stop. Flogging an idea to death is not only tiresome, it tends to obscure the idea. Not only is the second memo in figure 11.3 less emphatic, but the reader isn't entirely certain what it's about. Our own eloquence in these cases sometimes leads us astray: the more we say, the more there is to say. Many of us have heard sermons that were self-perpetuating (seemingly); the preacher keeps "being reminded" of something else on the same subject. The net effect of such verbosity isn't good: nobody listens. The same is true of letters, but more so. At least the preacher can talk about sin and miracles; all you're talking about in your business correspondence is widgets.

Grammatical Thoughts

Although we've discussed grammatical thoughts several times, we have yet to work out any usable guidelines for recognizing them. It's relatively easy to sort out absolute nonsense from obviously commonsensical statements:

Nonsense:　　　"'Twas brillig, and the slithy toves
　　　　　　　　　Did gyre and gimble in the wabe:
　　　　　　　　All mimsy were the borogroves,
　　　　　　　　　And the mome raths outgrabe."[2]
Commonsense:　"If you go long enough without a bath even
　　　　　　　　the fleas will let you alone."[3]

There's really no doubt about which of these is sensical and which isn't. No speaker of English would mistake the first example for grave, straightforward prose. Likewise, no one would mistake the second comment for lighthearted fantasy. Nevertheless, both examples are grammatically correct.

The reason that children (and the rest of us as well) delight in "Jabberwocky" is that it is grammatical. It sounds like it makes sense even though it doesn't. It summons up whatever images

---

2. *Lewis Carroll*, "Jabberwocky."
3. *Ernie Pyle*, Here Is Your War.

your mind will impose on those nonsense words, but few of us consider it worthless, ununderstandable garbage. Why? Because it doesn't fail to convey what it wants to convey: giggles.

On the other hand, read the following excerpt:

From Bogota you also can flight to Leticia 2,000 miles up the Amazon on the deep frontier with Peru and near Brazilian Border. Although it has grown from small settlement into a modern community of some 17,000 city. Good Hotel with frigid air and busty accomodations and sophisticated drinks make your holiday there something very comfortable. The jungle rugged outside. Rain, mosquitoes, nights horribly screams noises. The tourist could hardly hope to get closer to the jungle than there indians—male and feamale walk without cloth. River boats go and return to one side to another carrying merchandise to secrets indians villages, and conta band—corner of the three countries—is a sport like hunting crocodiles with a big stick. The womans that are impressive good looking in the whole territory of Colombia, here are limited and ugly. But you have beautiful monkey and colorful serpents; and thousand of magic and colorful birds, wall trees and mosquitoes.[4]

Now, there was no intention of conveying giggles here, but they erupt nonetheless. What other possible response is there to the author's "womans . . . limited and ugly" and "horribly screams noises"? The usages are so nonstandard that sense disappears, leaving behind nothing but a trail of meaningless words. The Colombian writer has obviously overstepped the boundaries of grammatical thoughts. His language lacks that quality that imparts sense to writing. His meaning is clouded, and sometimes completely obscured (what are "busty accomodations" and "wall trees"?). Although the example was chosen for its obvious hilarity, there's nothing funny about the following excerpt— which was written by and for American communicators.

Because the lagoon is subject to tides, because it has the appearance of being natural, because it is the source of water for the canals built northerly thereof, and because the portion northerly of the entrance channel has not been reclaimed, it is unclear what rights are retained by the owners of the fee and what rights, if any, may vest in the owners of property abutting the canals or in the general public.

---

4. From the ACC (Automobile Club of Colombia) magazine, quoted in The New Yorker, January 1978.

Looking back over these examples, we can begin to extrapolate some guidelines for grammatical thoughts. The first broad generalization we can make is that grammatical thoughts look like they make sense. The selection quoted above from "Jabberwocky" is nonsense, but the reader struggles to make it mean something because it looks like it ought to. What is the quality that makes something look sensical to the reader's eye? Simply put, it's standard usage.

Dictionaries and Such

The chief value of standardizing devices such as dictionaries is that they give us a norm to go by when interpreting other people's language. When a wife calls her husband at the office and asks him to bring home "a quart of milk," there's little doubt in his mind what her request is. Why? Because her request is phrased as a standard request, and because all the words in it are words in commonly accepted usage. When he buys a quart of homogenized whole milk and takes it home, he stands a good chance of complying exactly with her request. Now if the wife looks askance at his quart of milk, and tells him she thought he knew she meant a quart of low-fat milk, or a quart of raw milk, or a quart of acidophilus, or a quart of nondairy creamer—the couple has a problem.

Our eyes and ears are accustomed to certain types of sentences, to certain types of word definitions, and to certain types of logic. When these patterns are violated, we risk losing something in meaning. And, for some reason unknown to most of us, these patterns are violated with regularity and with purpose by the world of business and government. Standard grammar is simply ignored—not because it's difficult, but because the writer simply chooses to ignore it for better or worse.

A common violation of the rules of sense involves strings of nouns put together by committees to name themselves or their materials. What, in fact, could a "System Development Process Reference Guide" be? It could be a guide to provide reference material to those involved in the process of system development. It could be a guide to provide reference material on the process of development in a given system. It could be a guide to provide reference material concerning the various processes involved in the development of systems. It could be a person who acts as such a guide. There is, in fact, no way to tell exactly what it is from its name, but its name doesn't seem particularly outlandish in these days of rampant management science.

What is a "Dishonored Check Collector"? Is it perhaps a

person who failed at the job of collecting checks—and was drummed out of the organization minus his or her epaulets, brass buttons, and sword of office? Or is it just the everyday, humdrum person who searches out and puts together large collections of dishonored checks in albums printed for just such a purpose?

Grammatical thoughts (to return abruptly to the subject at hand) are thoughts put together in standard formats, using standard vocabulary with standard meanings, to convey the thought that appears to be intended. And the simpler they are, the better they are.

If you find that your sentences have a tendency to become a bit convoluted—or even just a bit long—pay more attention to the concept of grammatical thoughts. Try the following exercises, in sequence, for a week each:

Week One: Everything you write during this week must contain no word of more than three or four syllables. No fudging, please. You may be surprised at how many sentences you'll have to rework to comply—and at how much easier they are to read when you're finished.

Week Two: Now you are the master of the uncomplicated word. This week you must write no sentence more than ten words long. This is a very tough assignment, and to do it, you'll have to examine your thoughts carefully, sort them out into separate units, and phrase them with the utmost care and efficiency.

Week Three: Now for the most complicated of all exercises. This week you may write no paragraph of more than four sentences. No more than four, mind you—and that doesn't mean five.

By the time week four rolls around, you'll have learned as much as you need to know about grammatical thoughts. If you're still alive, that is.

Finding the Correct Medium

Once you've made your way through the perils of grammatical thoughts, you arrive at a stop on the communication path labeled "medium." It's the point at which you launch your message on its trek receiverward. The dangers you'll have to avoid here are particularly difficult ones—perhaps some that don't even occur to you in the course of everyday business. They have to do with your choice of medium. We've already discussed the many reasons not to write. What we'll do now is discuss the occasions when you must resort to writing. A good rule to follow is: "When all else fails, write."

Your best shot at conveying any message is a personal conversation face-to-face. You get immediate feedback in terms of body language, facial expressions, and, of course, words. Many times you can confirm whether your message was correctly received. And, considering that a full 70 percent of the paper that crosses the average desk is unnecessary, you have a much better chance of being heard than you have of being read. It's painfully obvious to most of us that we're drowning in a nationwide tidal wave of paper, and whatever we can do to reduce that disaster is a step in the right direction.

There are times when a personal conversation face-to-face isn't practical. But don't immediately pick up your pencil—try the telephone first. You trade off some things by using the phone, but it's still a better alternative than writing. You can still solicit immediate feedback, and you can roll with the punches. Once you've written something down, it's the devil's own job taking it back. But even the telephone isn't always practical, and there are times when writing is the only solution. Some of the times when you have no choice but writing include:

1. You have a request for a written report.
2. Your material would necessitate a phone call or conversation of a length that's out of the question.
3. Your material is highly technical or full of important data.
4. Your message is intended for someone who's unavailable by phone.
5. You don't know whom your message is intended for ("Attn: Customer Service or Repair Department").
6. Your message is intended for a multiple audience.
7. Cost dictates a written message rather than a personal one.
8. You need a written record of your message.

This list is by no means exhaustive; there are probably many other occasions when nothing but a written message will do. The point is that you should always try every alternative before you write. Never forget the following trade-offs:

1. When you write, you set up a one-way communication that generates no immediate feedback.
2. What you've written stays written and lingers in the files a lot longer than you might want it to.
3. Written messages can be passed around to people you might not expect.
4. A foolish written message is considerably more foolish than a foolish spoken message.

5. You are much less likely to make a grammatical garble of a spoken message than a written one.

And with those cheery provisos, we'll move on to the next chapter.

Exercises

1. To assess feedback from your writing, you need to set up some files. For each memo you write requesting a response or implying you need a response, set up a file. Put each response into the file. Do this for at least three of your memos. After sufficient time, review these files. Don't be horrified if you find very little response. You may not have communicated effectively. This will show you where to improve. You'll see how often and to what lengths you went to get a response.
2. In each of the cases in exercise 1, ask yourself if you've chosen the correct medium.
3. Look through recent reports generated by you or by members of your staff. Isolate at least four jargon phrases. See if each phrase can be misconstrued as the examples cited in this chapter can. Analyze each to determine if it can be clarified by developing a new phrase.
4. For a memo or letter, consciously write down the particles of meaning to be transferred. Pick a memo with at least five particles. If you followed up the chapter on decisions (chapter 5), then don't write down the various decisions. Order the particles in five different ways. Write a memo for each order of the particles. This will indicate the importance of order.
5. In the next week, attempt to reduce the amount of writing you do to the bare minimum. This can be done through deferral of writing as well as through the use of oral communication.

12
Managing for Good Communications

What can American business do to improve the overall quality of business communication? First of all, of course, each member of the business community can endeavor to improve his skills in transmitting messages adequately and accurately. Second, each person can try to receive messages as they were intended, applying the principles we evolved in chapter 10. But we really can't expect to improve overall communication by improving the skills of all the individuals involved. There are too many of them, and their motivations and abilities vary too widely. So we must find some ways in which management can encourage better communication.

As faulty as it frequently is, communication in American business is adequate to the large needs of the business community. Business does progress; product is sold; capital does move. It won't always be so. If the communication skills of businesspeople continue to decline at the current rate, we'll shortly find ourselves backsliding in productivity. That's already the case in some companies, particularly ones that have grown so rapidly that good communication systems have not yet been created. Take the case of a small petrochemicals company headquartered in Houston. For the sake of anonymity, we call them XYZ Oil and Gas—but the case study is real.

XYZ is a capital-rich company; its backers have what is, for all practical purposes, unlimited capital for investment. They have only three offices: the home office in Houston, a sales office in Los Angeles, and a sales office in New York.

XYZ is a petroleum and petroleum products broker; it

locates and buys oil and oil fractions for its customers. Each of its offices has both a sales function and a product function. Because of the circumstances of the petroleum market, there are strict corporate rules about extending credit—at least on paper.

For the past three years, the Los Angeles office, headed by George Tate, has seemed to set its own rules on credit. Tate is knowledgeable in the field, and his customers are cleared for ability to pay on his personal say-so. The home office in Houston has attempted, from time to time, to tighten up the reins on Tate's operation, but has stopped short of a real management showdown.

Now a management audit conducted by the parent corporation has demanded a halt to Tate's easy-credit policy, and has mandated Houston to collect all amounts owing in excess of credit limits and past contractual pay dates. Bob Miller, a vice-president in charge of commercial development, has been assigned the sticky task of cleaning up Tate's mess in Los Angeles.

Miller and the president of XYZ, John Barber, put their heads together and write a no-nonsense memorandum to Tate, informing him of corporate policy on credit and on outstanding receivables. Miller delivers the memorandum in person. Tate sits down, reads the memorandum, and replies, simply, "That's not the way we do things here."

XYZ is faced with a problem it has not foreseen: either it must remove Tate (which will effectively close down the Los Angeles operation), or it must continue to bend the rules in Tate's direction. The decision is made to fire Tate.

This may not seem to be a communication problem—just a conflict of personalities and policies. It is, in fact, a communication problem almost purely. Here are the components:

1. Policy has been ignored in the past, invalidating—in Tate's eyes—the words contained in the corporate policy manual.
2. Tate's image in his customers' eyes includes a facet that really doesn't belong to him: credit manager. XYZ has never set up a formal credit relationship with its customers in the Los Angeles region. If this image is altered suddenly and drastically, Tate will suffer severe loss of face.
3. Houston has (albeit reluctantly) opted for a showdown with Tate on the issue—a "no win" situation for Tate.

Figure 12.1 shows the flow of information in the Houston versus Tate situation.

The setup is typical of a young and dynamic company. Each person is accustomed to wearing several hats, and no communication lines are duplicated anywhere. The parent corporation doesn't communicate with Tate; Houston doesn't communicate

Figure 12.1. Communication lines—XYZ Corporation.

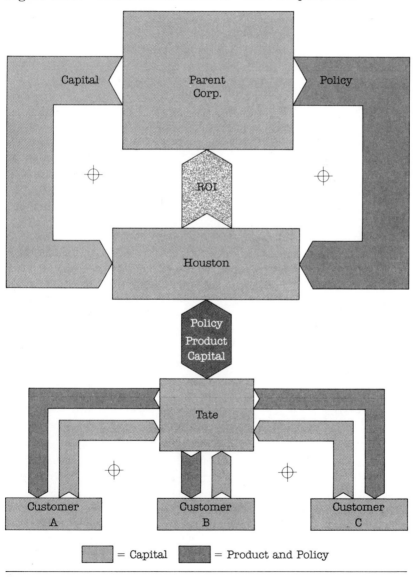

with Tate's customers. Older and wiser corporations don't work this way. A more typical setup for larger operations is pictured in figure 12.2.

Notice that communications have been set up quite differently in 12.2, as they are dictated by business needs. Under this plan, Tate (who is essentially a sales officer) has no connection with

Figure 12.2. Communication lines—XYZ Corporation (revised).

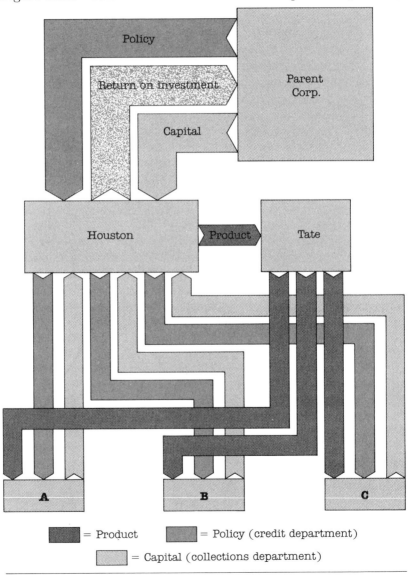

credit or collections. And note that, under this plan, there's no possibility of a showdown with Tate, because the subject in question bypasses him completely.

In terms of the communication path, what's the difference between the two communication systems? The problem is with the flow of capital and policy. Look at figure 12.3 for an analysis of the current XYZ organization; figure 12.4 visualizes the communications of the organization pictured in figure 12.2.

What all these diagrams are meant to illustrate is that XYZ Corporation would do well in future to differentiate between the types of messages it intends to send to its clients and to find the most efficient path for each message separately. If Houston is to be responsible for credit and collections, it shouldn't be put in the position of having to speak through Tate to Tate's clients. If Tate

Figure 12.3   Communication Path Analysis—XYZ Corporation.

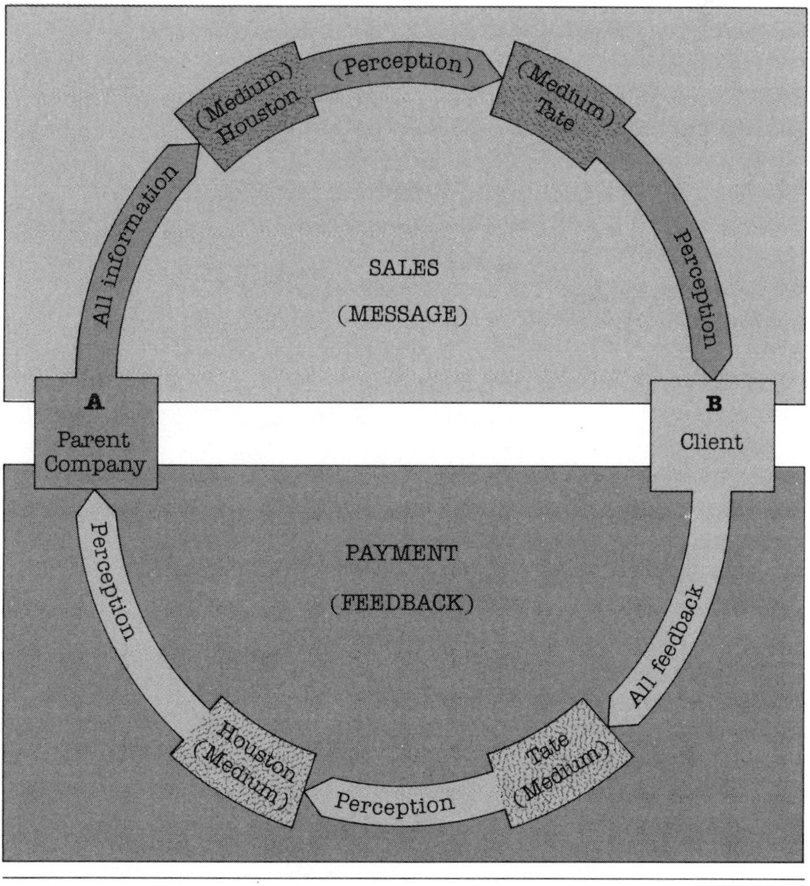

Figure 12.4.   Communication Path Analysis—XYZ Corporation
(revised).

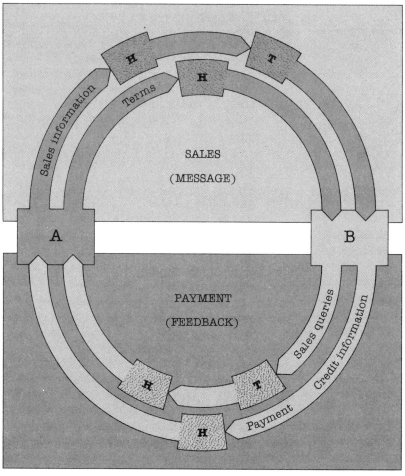

is to have no meaningful say-so in opening lines of credit, he
shouldn't be burdened with carrying credit messages from
Houston. This simple case follows two old qualifiers for sales
clients:

need or interest in the product
ability to pay

Without one or the other, of course, you have either no sale or a
bad sale. Since XYZ Corporation is pleased with Tate as a salesman, but concerned with his performance as a pseudo credit

manager, they might have avoided the showdown by simply rearranging the lines of communication. Certainly if they reopen the Los Angeles office after the Tate affair cools down, they should consider a reorganization along these lines.

The troubles at XYZ are indicative of two major types of communication problems prevalent in today's business world:

1. devalued messages
2. diverted messages

Devalued Messages

Saying one thing and meaning another can be a dangerous business. Parenting handbooks warn against hollow threats in rearing children: never tell a child you intend to punish him when you don't intend to follow through. In that sense, parenting handbooks should be applied rigorously to everyday business.

In politics, ethics, and morals, we call it hypocrisy. In business, it's called by various names such as "bending the rules." But they are simply a variety of names for one type of offense. What is the danger of hypocrisy? For one thing, it makes the words that convey it meaningless; it has a serious effect on future communication from the same source. Like the boy who cried "Wolf!" the Houston office of XYZ has a hard time making Tate believe that this time they mean business.

What's the practical application of the XYZ lesson? It's simply that using a communication channel for worthless or meaningless messages devalues the entire validity of the channel. If I call a client every day and have nothing to say, he'll no longer be listening to me when I do have something to say.

The flood of useless paper that engulfs business today vastly overloads the channels of communication, and the end effect of this tsunami of memos and bulletins and letters and reports is much the same as an endless cry of "Wolf!" Regardless of whether the information in the continuous stream of paper is valid, readers have ceased to pay attention to certain types of it. Employees in large corporations, for example, almost never read personnel bulletins, because they're typically confusing and unimportant. Consequently, employee relations departments find that their really important messages are frequently missed. Think back on the last three memos you got from employee relations— do you even remember what they were about? Did you read them?

Devalued messages are messages to which nobody pays any attention. In the case of XYZ, Houston's messages about credit rules were completely devalued by their continuing unwillingness to enforce what was acknowledged to be company policy.[1] In the case of the ignored employee relations correspondence, it is simply a matter of being battered to death by useless official paper; one ceases to care what it says. In a third common case, messages are devalued by putting them into certain kinds of professional jargon, such as legalese. Unless a legalese message is frightening, it will probably be ignored, because the language alienates the reader and devalues the message.

Diverted Messages

A diverted message is simpler to understand, but every bit as difficult to root out. It is a message that is sent through the wrong channel or the wrong medium—and it loses meaning and importance in the diversion.

In the XYZ case, the messages concerning credit were diverted by routing them through Tate, who had no authority to deal with them. Tate thought that since he was being included in the chain of command regarding credit, he had some authority in the matter. He was, after all, the only line of communication XYZ had with its Los Angeles area customers. A possible solution to the diversion would involve Tate's bringing in the credit department for clearance—before product was cleared to be shipped. If Houston is unwilling to delegate credit clearance authority to Tate, it shouldn't burden him with the duty of administering a company policy that clearly conflicts with his instincts as a salesman (at least in his view).

One of the most disastrous—and common—diverted messages involves personnel departments that recruit new employees. It's becoming a common practice for employee relations staff members to interview job applicants for a wide variety of positions that may be open. The situation created isn't practical; it's unfair both to the company and to the job applicant. You cannot ask a person with a background in industrial relations to screen applicants for jobs in fields he knows nothing about—at least you cannot ask it and hope to get the best results. By diverting job applications to an employee relations department, you create a communication path like the one in figure 12.5. Notice that it has severe drawbacks in the entire area known as "language" on the path.

---

1. *Official policy is frequently the victim of such devaluation; it is ignored widely. Why? It is sometimes out of date, sometimes unenforceable, sometimes impractical. Why does it continue to be policy? Because, in its devalued state, it's not worth the effort to change it—nobody would pay any attention anyway.*

Figure 12.5. Personnel department—job application function.

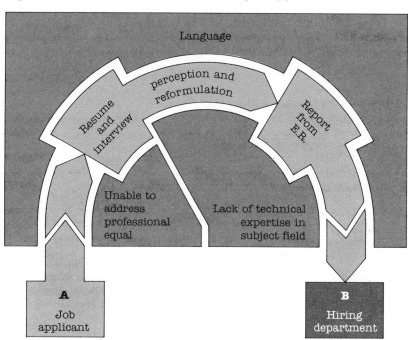

Diverted messages present two major problems for business:

1. They lose accuracy and dependability by being strained through an uninformed or uninterested medium.

2. They encourage the development of territorial empires that serve no real purpose. The easiest of these empires to identify is the personnel department whose only real function is to pass messages back and forth between employees and management. The product of such a go-between department is a bureaucracy of secrets and policy, a vested interest in maintaining problems (or creating them), and a substantial addition to overhead cost.

What's to Be Done?

The first step is for management to realize that technology isn't a cure. You cannot buy any gadget that will prevent communication foul-ups. In fact, most communication technology intensifies whatever breakdowns are present.

For business to improve the overall level of communication proficiency, it must recognize that communication is a human (not a machine) function. Good communication—that is, communication that conveys meaning correctly—can be immensely enhanced by useful gadgets and machines. For example, it's much easier to discuss a blueprint on the telephone if one party to a conversation can use a facsimile machine to send emendations and corrections to the other. That same facsimile machine can be no help at all if the two parties involved in the communication are unskilled or uninvolved or careless in what they say or write. If I can't use the right words in a letter, there's no reason to believe I'll be able to find the right words for a telex. If I can't explain a graph on a mimeographed handout, I won't be able to explain the same graph on a 70mm superslide.

Good communication can be built into any organization by attention to two factors: the people and the system. If, for example, you were to hire new employees with a real eye to communication skills, you'd have a chance of upgrading the overall level of communication skills in your company. There are some practical, easy-to-administer tests for writing skills. If you find it permissible to test potential secretaries for typing speed, isn't it then equally permissible to test new middle management types for literacy?

The colleges and universities turn out exactly the type of student they think will be easily absorbed into the job marketplace. Since none of the major companies seems to care much about the level of communication skills in new employees, those skills have been de-emphasized in schools. Foreign language studies, which used to be the single best teacher of English language structure, are no longer either recommended or required at most universities. And it's common knowledge that today's college graduate isn't a proficient reader or writer.

However, if business were to begin administering literacy tests to potential employees, we'd certainly find the emphasis shifting in the colleges to accommodate that trend. Here's a simple literacy test which should prove very revealing to potential employers:

> Ask the job applicant to write a single paragraph describing a simple object—say a thumbtack. It doesn't take long for the applicant to write it, or for the employer to read it. It is not a test of creative skills, but a test of observation, logic, and organization. Anyone who can fully describe a thumbtack in one paragraph is reasonably literate. The literacy level is easily determined by the employer—if you can understand what was written, the applicant passes the test. A surprising number of

recent college graduates cannot pass such a simple test, and it's helpful to employers to weed those people out during the hiring process. After all, anyone who manages to get through sixteen years of school without learning to write isn't likely to develop decent writing skills during his first few years on the job.

Upgrading Current Employees

As we've emphasized over and over in this book, writing is an acquired skill. And, like other essential management skills, it benefits from well-planned refresher training courses. There are a variety of training courses available in business writing. Some are offered in connection with colleges and universities; others are available as in-house courses of varying lengths. The local branch of the American Society for Training and Development (ASTD) should be able to provide a list of courses available in your area.

Whatever course is chosen for your company's use, it should have the following components:

1.   a substantial amount of in-class writing—on a variety of challenging subjects[2]
2.   individual feedback to each class participant on areas of real or potential concern

There's no way a writing class can be effective as a series of lectures. Writing is a manual and mental skill; you could as soon and as reasonably expect to learn to play the violin from lectures as to improve your writing that way.

When scheduling writing courses, remember that the good communicators in your organization will benefit from them as much as the poor communicators. Placing tangible emphasis on communication skills in job advancement will also help upgrade current levels of competence. If an employee is evaluated in his yearly salary review on the basis of communication skills (along with whatever other criteria are germane), she'll be motivated to improve.

Improving the Files

Just as the quality of your memory affects the quality of your writing, the quality and accessibility of your company's files affects the level of communication among employees. Nothing, for instance, causes more excess paperwork than bad files. How? If

---

2.   *It's the opinion of the authors that nonbusiness subjects offer the best, least-threatening practice in writing techniques.*

you can't locate information or don't know where to look for it, you must ask someone else to help you find it. In that fashion, many companies experience the transfer of the same bits and pieces of information—through the same channels—over and over again.

Some forward-looking companies have undertaken the Herculean task of standardizing files companywide. Under such a system, all files are ordered numerically under a master index. No matter which department you're in or which file cabinet you look into, all the information on a particular subject is filed under the same file heading. If, for example, departments A, B, and C all have an interest in OSHA regulations, they'll all file their OSHA material under the same decimal heading. If department C wants to query department A on the subject, they can ask for files numbered (for example) 12.2 through 12.4 and know that they'll get the right information.

What's the difference between that system and the usual system? In most companies, each department devises its own filing system. More accurately put, a filing system grows in each department—with no particular, discernible pattern. And under that nonsystem, there is no dependable way in which department A can query department C about anything. If the secretary who filed the latest OSHA report decided it belonged under S for "Safety," then that's where it is. If he decided to file it under O for "OSHA," then that's where it is—and so on. It might even be filed under F because it came with a cover letter from John Frank.

And, if you can't locate the particles of meaning you want to transfer to someone, you can't begin to put a message together.

Limiting the Flow of Paper

The most important thing any manager can do to improve communication is to discourage unnecessary paperwork. That's a difficult task, because most white-collar workers feel that they're judged by the quantity of paperwork they generate. Since white-collar workers seldom produce a product other than paper, they're extremely attached to paper. They send out reams of carbon copies of their letters and reports—simply to let their superiors and cohorts know they're there. The effect of such a tendency is to flood offices with unnecessary paper and, conse-quently, to devalue the important messages along with the unimportant. As long as the measures of an employee's impor-tance are the size of the stack of paper in his in and out baskets and the number of carbon-copy lists he's on, there's no hope for limiting paperwork.

Unfortunately, there's no easy way to decrease the amount of paper your office generates. Sometimes weekly meetings are a help; other times weekly meetings simply generate more paper: minutes, responses to queries, and so on. It's a matter of management style. If managers tend to judge the quality of output by the quantity of paper, then quantity of paper is what they'll get. If managers want all employees to look busy all the time, employees will figure out projects to keep them busy—and somehow those projects all seem to relate to paper in the end.

There's a simple test to determine the extent of unnecessary paperwork that crosses your desk. Don't file anything for a week. At the end of the week, look through the stacks of paper on your desk. The paper you haven't read and the paper you don't intend to read is all unnecessary. In most offices, that unnecessary paper makes up nearly 80 percent of the week's mail.

In contemplating that solitary statistic, it is well to keep in mind that one of the marks of a good communicator is knowing when to keep silent.

Exercises

1. This exercise is intended to test your filing system. Select subjects that cut across the files. Determine the effort needed to retrieve the information.
2. In doing exercise 1, go through your office and files and delete as many of the files and file entries as possible.
3. Assume you're in a staff position in a large corporation. The corporation is decentralized into autonomous divisions. You have been told to collect information from the divisions on their use and projected use of data processing equipment. Develop an approach for identifying names of contact points.
4. In the situation in exercise 3, determine the format and approach for initial contact with the divisions.
5. For the situation in exercise 3, develop a framework for collecting data. Discuss the appropriateness of a questionnaire.
6. For exercises 4 and 5, discuss how the messages could be diverted.

Special Section: Using Communication Skills to Get That Job

With all your skills and knowledge, you're hard-pressed to put forth your best effort if you don't like your job—or if you don't have a job. And since few of us are really trained in getting a job, the task presents itself as uninviting.

Midcareer changes are more the rule than the exception these days. Companies are more and more interested in people with varied backgrounds, and employees are less and less interested in spending their entire careers in the same company. The fortunate few who are sought after by management placement agencies (headhunters) are only the top of the iceberg of traveling managers. The business world constantly profits from the experience of its employees—and some of the most successful managers are those whose backgrounds are the most checkered.

Most employees will find themselves in the position of looking for a job sooner or later. This chapter presents a practical and helpful technique.

Over whatever period you've been working, you've put together a certain amount of experience in doing specific things. Traditional wisdom would have it that you take that experience, arrange it, and produce a resume. Voila! Then what do you do? You set up some job interviews (as if that were easy), and you select the employer who's right for you. Somehow the real world just isn't like that. There are snags, unforeseen complications, very real personal problems.

Basically, there are two situations in which people look for jobs:

1. You're out of work (fired, quit, whatever).
2. You're currently employed, but looking for something better (or different)—whether that search is in-house or at other corporations.

Each situation has its own frustrations and its own complications.

As everyone knows, "nobody knows you when you're down and out." The everyday corollary to that famous lyric is nobody wants to hire someone who's unemployed. There are exceptions, of course, but they're surprisingly few. Usually, if your resume doesn't list a current occupation, you get a squint-eyed, slit-mouthed, disbelieving stare from the person interviewing you. You know they suspect you were "fired for cause." You begin to feel a bit inferior, because the American ethic says if you really want to work (you bum), you'll be able to find work. If you're out of work (you worthless, good-for-nothing lump), there's more than likely something wrong with you. You know that as well as the interviewer does, and you feel obliged to defend yourself.

Then, of course, there are the doldrums in an unsatisfactory position. You know very well you want out—and up—but the pay is decent, and the work doesn't really *bother* you. You have friends there, and somehow you find that your career is taking backseat to something you can't even pinpoint. Call it inertia. And, besides, your boss may not take it kindly if he finds out you're shopping.

What Do You Do First?

The first step is the same for each of the two cases mentioned above. It's the most difficult thing in life, but it must be done if you're to find a job that's suitable and rewarding. Socrates said it first, but it's still powerful advice: know yourself.

Platitudes, platitudes, platitudes. Right? Wrong. The only thing that can give you the confidence and the energy you need to land the right position is a thorough knowledge of yourself—who you are, what you can do, and where you're going. If you know the answers to these things—not just vaguely or intuitively, but concretely—then you'll know as well that there's a job out there waiting for you.

We're not talking hype or Dale Carnegie positive-thinking spiels, although they have their place in any sales endeavor (and when you're job-hunting, you're selling yourself). We're talking about solid, step-by-step, self-knowledge. The first thing you have to do when job hunting is to conduct a very pointed self-interview.

How to Interview Yourself

We spoke earlier about interviewing someone else: writing goals, conducting the interview, hardware needed, and so on. It's very much the same for a self-interview. The first thing you need to compile is a set of interview goals. We're in a position to give you some assistance. There are three large questions you must put to yourself:

1. Who are you?
2. Who are you going to be?
3. Who were you in the past?

Three easy little questions that can turn your psyche upside down. But don't try job hunting until you have the answers, because you'll find nothing there but failure—in the form of a job you don't like or of no job at all.

Notice that we've listed the questions in an order that isn't chronological. We're asking you to work from the present to the future and then from the future to the past. There's method in it: if someone's going to hire you, they're going to hire you *as you are*, not as you were. They may well hire you for what you're going to be, but their idea of what you're going to be will be based solidly on what you are today. How do you decide who you are?

Who Are You?

The first thing to decide is that you're you and not someone else. There are in excess of four billion people in the world and no two are alike. You're unlike anyone else in the world. That's a truism and a cliche, but it's also an absolute. If you treat yourself as a member of a class of people—undistinguishable from the others —you move several rungs down the ladder of job possibilities. Throughout the process of self-interviewing, remember that you're looking for the differences between you and everyone else—as well as for the similarities.

As an employable person, you have two sides: an individual side (which makes you different), and a group side (which makes your particular skills usable in a variety of organizations). Let's work first on the group side. Ask yourself this simple question: Who am I? Answer it in terms of a job category:

1. I'm an accountant.
2. I'm a salesman.
3. I'm an administrator.
4. I'm a chemical engineer.
5. I'm a historian.

Write down your answer.

Consider yourself as having in life, as you had in college, a major and a minor; the answer to the first question was your major field of concentration. Now ask yourself the same question (who am I?) and exclude the first answer from all the possible answers in the world. Find yourself a minor (or a few minors).

Example A
A person has answered, "I am an administrator," to the first phrasing of "Who am I?" The second round of answers might include some of the following:

1. I'm (also) an expert on organization and compensation.
2. I'm (also) a personnel recruiter.
3. I'm (also) an office manager.

Example B
A person has answered, "I'm a chemical engineer," to the first phrasing of "Who am I?" The second round of answers might include some of the following:

1. I'm (also) an administrator or manager.
2. I'm (also) a project leader.
3. I'm (also) particularly knowledgeable in hydrocarbons.

When you have the answers to the major and minor aspects of the question, "Who am I?" you have a necessary beginning to your task. You've identified some of your salable skills—some of the things that make you the *same* as other people in the job market. Now note down for yourself some of the evidence you'd use to prove these answers to a potential employer. Forget college degrees (unless college is your most recent experience), and concentrate on the present. The answers might include something like:

1. I've been employed for three years as a chemical engineer in a polyethylene plant. ("I'm a chemical engineer.")

2. I had three employees reporting to me. ("I'm also an administrator.")
3. I had planning control of two important projects. ("I'm a project leader.")
4. My most recent experience has been heavily involved with petroleum hydrocarbons at XYZ Chemicals. ("I'm particularly knowledgeable in hydrocarbons.")

So far the process sounds like a normal makeready for compiling a resume, doesn't it? It is similar in some ways, but we've been operating from a different vantage point, and the information will be more selective and more useful. Normally, in compiling a resume, you'd ask yourself questions more like:

1. "What was my most recent (current) job?"
2. "What was my job title and description?"

The answers to questions like those two are more descriptive of the organization for which you've been working than of yourself. And, if you proceed from questions like those, you'll have trouble at the resume-writing stage. You'll find yourself making statements like, "I was a Chemical Engineer Stage 2, which at XYZ means. . . ." And nobody is going to hire you on the basis of what Stage 2 meant at XYZ.

Figure 1 illustrates what you've accomplished so far in terms of identifying yourself. Now that you've identified yourself

Figure 1. Identifying yourself.

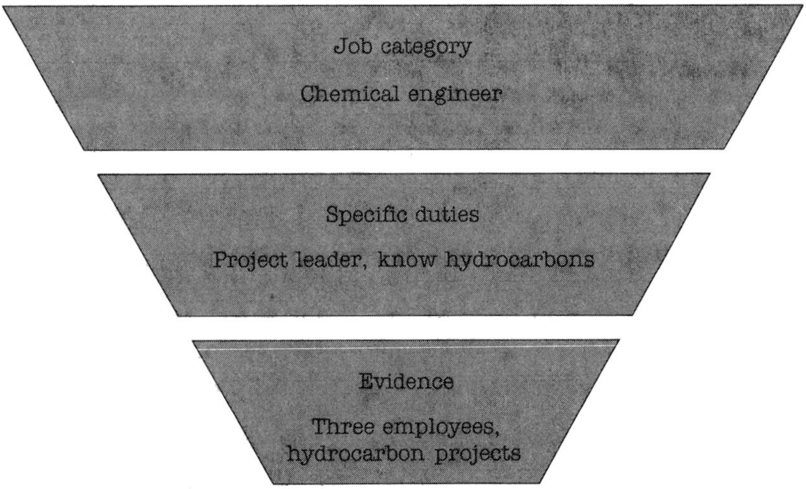

Job category
Chemical engineer

Specific duties
Project leader, know hydrocarbons

Evidence
Three employees,
hydrocarbon projects

(and the more soulsearching you do, the better that identification will be), you're ready to move on to the next step in the interview.

Who Are You Going to Be?

If you're applying for a job as anything other than a hack, your employer is going to be interested—mightily interested—in what you consider to be your future progress. If you've ever interviewed for a job, you already know the question, "Where do you think your career is taking you?" It's a difficult question to answer on the spot, and on-the-spot answers are frequently wishy-washy and unimpressive:

"I hope to be working in a job that's responsible and challenging."
"I want to move into management."
"I'm looking for a position with possibilities for promotion."
"I want my job to be a learning experience."

There's virtually no end to the platitudes that the mind can come up with in response to the simple question, "Who are you going to be?" What's wrong with answering in tried-and-true sentiments like the ones listed? They do contain an element of truth, don't they? Of course there's truth in any platitude; that's why it has become a platitude. What's wrong with it in an interview is that it's imprecise and nondescript. There are two main evils to be seen in answers like those:

1. An insecure interviewer may think you're going to be after his job the minute he hires you.
2. Any interviewer hears junk like this all day. He won't be able to remember your answer. You'll seem like just one more vaguely ambitious applicant. And without individuality, you're not likely to be distinguishable from the great mass of unwashed applicants interviewed before and after you.

What you have to do is figure out a way to supply some answers with a bit more pizzazz—a bit more flare and a bit more character. The translation of those descriptions is simply this: you have to be concrete, reasonable, and in line with your current identity. So what you're striving for in this segment of the interview is precision applied to concrete ideas. Everybody likes a person who knows his own mind, and, if you interview yourself properly, you'll find out some things you never knew before about yourself.

The method we'll use is the same as the method we used to

determine who you are today. First, out of all the possible occupations in the world, you must pick one as the primary answer to the simple question, "Who are you going to be?" There are two ways to go: either you want to stay in your current occupation (although perhaps at a higher level) or you want to move into something else. In the case of our chemical engineer, possible answers might include the following:

1. I'll still be a chemical engineer.
2. I'll be a new-product researcher.
3. I'll be an administrator.
4. I'll be a management development trainer.
5. I'll be an independent consultant.
6. I'll be a chemical librarian.

Note two things about this list: (a) all the answers bear a relationship to the answers this person made to the question about her current identity; and (b) some of the answers may preclude long-term employment at the company to which she is applying. The ambition to be an independent consultant certainly precludes regular employment; and very few companies are large enough to employ a full-time chemical librarian.

Despite the fact that some of these answers dictate a feeling of short-term employment, each of them is a valid—and acceptable —answer to use in the context of a resume. Don't worry about whether the employer you're talking to can provide a niche; be true to yourself. If you're true to yourself and a valuable employee to boot, an employer may well find a niche that doesn't currently exist when the time comes. An interviewer would have to be remarkably blind to exclude all possible applicants who want someday to consult, for instance; and the fact is that many independent consultants maintain healthy, mutually beneficial relationships with their former employers.

Once you have an answer to the question, "Who are you going to be?" you're ready to look for some subsidiary answers—as before. Exclude the answer you've just made from the world of possible answers, and go for a few more. Let's continue with the example of our chemical engineer, and let's presume that she had decided that she'll be an administrator (number three in the list of possibilities). Her minor answers might look like some of these:

1. I'll still be a chemical engineer.
2. I'll be recruiting new, talented employees.
3. I'll be helping to develop new products.

A picture of the applicant begins to emerge from these ambitions—even though they're as yet unsupported by evidence. And a clear, well-defined picture is the applicant's best asset. It's the only thing that will make him stand out from the herd of bovine creatures who send in traditional resumes for every job in the newspaper.

Now that we have a list of "futures," we're ready to substantiate them. Pick a piece of evidence for each of them (concentrating most heavily, of course, on the major) from the following list:

1. Your ongoing formal education.
2. Parts of previous jobs.
3. Long-standing ambitions (as long as they aren't ridiculous).
4. Proven aptitudes.
5. Areas you've worked in that are tangential.

Don't include evidence that falls under the following:

"Everyone has always said I should be a . . ."
"Since I take on responsibility well . . ."
"Since I work well with people . . ."

In other words, don't use any evidence that isn't both concrete and specific. Vague ambitions are unsettling—much more un-settling than ambitions that are too lightly supported. After all, when you have a specific goal in mind, your employer can devise a development plan for you if you merit it. If your goal rests on a statement like, "I've always liked people—I'm really a people person," he has to decide what you are before he can even think about developing you into something else.

Now you have two lists: (a) who you are and (b) who you will be. Both are supported by evidence. Time to move on.

Who Were You in the Past?

You've probably already noticed that the past is well represented on the resume before we even consider it. All (or most) of your evidence is drawn from the past (the past starts today and includes all history before today). So you've got a head start on this part of the interview.

As you might guess, we'll use the same approach to the past that we've used with the present and the future. You must generate a major and several minor answers to the question, "Who were you in the past?" In answering the questions in this section, be certain you don't show a background unrelated to the future. Even if you're making a midcareer change that's radical, you must show a semblance of continuity in your life to avoid looking unstable. How do you do this and remain true to the facts and to yourself? Easy: You simply arrange the evidence from most important to least important on the basis of its relationship to the future. Let's assume that our chemical engineer has made the following answers to the question, "Who were you in the past?"

Major: I was a petroleum refining specialist.
Minor: 1. I was an above-average student.
2. I was a lab assistant.
3. I was a college basketball player.

Each of those four answers must be made to show a relationship to the future, or it must be replaced by something else. It can be done:

Statement	Evidence
I was a petroleum refining specialist.	previous job experience
I was an above-average student.	degrees; honors
I was a lab assistant.	college employment
I was a college basketball player.[1]	competitive spirit, outgoing, results-oriented sportsperson willing to sweat for goals.

You now have three lists: present, future, and past. You're ready to begin work on a resume.

What Is a Resume?

A resume is half a document. It's never used (properly) by itself. It should always be accompanied by one of the following:

a letter
an application
an interview

Consequently, it should be composed as half a document. That is to say, it must be organized to complement a letter or application

---

1. *Notice the explanation of having been a basketball player. No chemical engineer is going to be hired on the basis of how well he or she plays basketball, but one may be hired on the basis of what we have listed as evidence. In the case of the past, evidence can include whatever you want it to include—as long as it supports the future (and as long as it's true).*

fully. It must be easy to lead into; it must be organized for visual ease; it must be a reference tool that your potential employer can see represents you to a tee.

What's the practical application of what we've just said? Most important, a resume must be well and formally organized. We recommend a standard, formal outline format—with major headings underlined and all major thoughts numbered. Certainly each position you've held should be numbered, so that you can refer in your letter to "number 4 on the attached resume."

Remember that resume reading is a gruesome chore. Imagine that you're an employer and you've advertised a position in the newspaper; you've received forty-five resumes in response. Are you going to read them all? If you read them, how are you going to remember them? Tell them apart? The task of resume reading must be made as easy as possible. That in itself will help make your resume memorable, because most resumes are as opaque as india ink and as boring as yesterday's oatmeal.

Writing a resume is a writing task no different in its basics from other writing tasks. It's the writer's responsibility to convey the message to the reader. In the case of resumes, the reading audience is apt to be a particularly uninterested, rushed person untrained in reading resumes. The reader does have a responsibility to himself and to his company to read carefully and thoroughly through all the resumes he receives. Unfortunately in the real world, it just doesn't happen that way.

Resume Format

There are some traditions in resume writing worth noting. Some ought to be adhered to closely; others are optional. In any case, your resume must be a picture of you; anything that helps you enhance that picture of yourself should be seriously considered. If any of these rules seem inappropriate to you, discard them. Generally there are six sections of a good resume:

1. personal data
2. current employment
3. previous employment
4. awards, honors, publications
5. more personal data
6. references

1. Personal Data   There are laws that prohibit your prospective employer from asking personal questions about you. And those laws are sensible, necessary methods of assuring nondiscrimination in employment. It's wise, nonetheless, to provide some personal information to the person who reads your resume. Why? Because if you're hired, you'll be hired as a person. If you're remembered, it will be as a person. If you have no identity in your resume, you'll simply fall into the mass of resumes to be considered—and the resumes with flair, individuality, and personality will have the edge over you. What kinds of personal data should you include? Any of the following with which you're comfortable: age, educational background, marital status, health, willingness to relocate, physical description (height, weight, color of eyes and hair). If none of the above are easy for you, then either figure out something else or omit this section. Many employers will appreciate some sort of statement about your education; this is the place to put it in.

2. *Current Employment*   Give the name, address, and phone of your current employer, together with the identity of your current supervisor. Include a brief description of your job, using active verbs and simple language. Concentrate on the evidence you decided on to bolster your three identities (past, present, and future). Be sure to include in this section a statement about whether your current employer can be contacted for references.

3. *Previous Employment*   Give names, addresses, and phone numbers of all previous employers. Account for all time elapsed since you left school, but avoid using the term *unemployed.* Try to keep your job descriptions brief and active. No description should be longer than your description of your current position, and no description should be longer than one that appears above it. Jobs you held ten years ago or more can be listed with only a job title. Again, be certain to concentrate on the evidence you decided on during your personal self-interview.

4. *Awards, Honors, Publications*   Preference here is for awards received during your working life. If you have none, feel free to use awards and activities earned during school, if school is relatively recent. If you have no entries, don't feel bad—most people don't. It's a plus if you do, but it's no big deal if your resume simply doesn't have this section.

5. *More Personal Data*   Note that we're advising you to begin and end your resume with a description of you as an individual. The statements in this section should differ from the personal data at the beginning of the resume in that the picture conveyed here is one of you as you relate to your industry and the community around you. Choose from the following list of possibilities, or add some of your own: professional associations or clubs, community or educational (but not religious)

organizations, foreign languages, hobbies or special interests, charitable memberships. In addition, we recommend including a snapshot of yourself with any mailed resume. The best way of including such a photo is to have your resume printed with a photo in the upper right corner of the first page. The purpose is, again, to mark you as a person distinct from all others. If your resume has a photo on it, chances are it will be the only one read that does. That singles you out—which can only be a plus. If you aren't photogenic, use a photo that is obviously a home snapshot. If you can't decide which one to use, ask someone else to decide. If you can't bear the idea, forget it.

The resume in figure 2 follows all these rules, and can be used as a model. Notice that the references are mentioned in only one line at the bottom of the second page. No names are given. We prefer to see references included in the letter that introduces the resume, but they must be mentioned on the resume itself.

Figure 2. Sample resume.

John Jones
519 Selby
Los Angeles, Calif. 90071
(213) 825-2502

1. Personal Data

Marital Status:	Single	Height:	6' 3"
Health:	Excellent	Weight:	175 lbs.
Age:	35	Eyes:	Brown
Willing to Relocate		Hair:	Brown

Education:
   B.A., Sitmar State College, Accounting, 1969
   M.B.A., University of Redondo, Finance, 1971

2. Current Employment

Senior Loan Officer, State Bank, Western Branch, 4044 S. Western, (213) OX6-7249, R. Smith (supervisor), 1977–present.
a. Investigate and approve all business loans for branch region.
b. Supervise seven staff members.
c. Complete department budgets.

3. Previous Employment

    A. 1973–1977: Loan Officer, Southern Savings, 545 S. State St., Santa Maria, CA., (809) 455-8207.
Assisted manager in generating and processing commercial loans. Handled customer contact on loans from three major ongoing clients—heavy industry.
    B. 1971–1973: Loan Officer, Southern Savings, 825 Montgomery St., San Francisco, (415) 827-3305.
Interviewed new clients, processed loan requests.

4. Awards, Honors

1965 Man of Year, Junior Guides of America.

5. Other Personal Data

Organizer, Western Recreation Group, 1972–present.
Member, Executive Business Association, 1974–1977.
Working knowledge of French, Italian.
Hobbies and Sports—stamp collecting, handball, jogging.

Note as well that no salary figures are included on the resume. If a salary history is required by the potential employer, treat it in your letter; it's a good way of relating the letter to the resume. In no case should more than two salary figures be included: a previous figure and the current figure.[2]

The Other Half

We've already said that a resume is only half a document. Now we're going to add the sad truth that it's the less important half. Why? Picture yourself as a person looking for a new employee. You receive a reply to your newspaper ad; it's composed of a one-page letter and a two-page resume. Which do you read first? The letter, of course. If the letter doesn't interest you, you may never get to the resume. If the letter is impressive, solid, and brief, you may have made up your mind about the candidate before you ever get to the resume. Because it's the letter that gets first attention, it's the letter that's the more important of the two components.

---

2. *There's a school of thought that says the current figure should be calculated on the basis of salary plus benefits. If you use this formula, be sure to make the reader aware that you have used it: "I figure that my current earnings, including benefits, fall into the range of . . ."*

Look back at the discussion of Marie Collins's search for a job (pages 27–30). We presumed that Marie would have a resume, but it's on the basis of her letter of introduction that she'll either enter or drop out of the running. Most employers are more accustomed to reading letters than resumes—they simply relate better to letter-type prose. Resumes are an unusual writing (and reading) format. Your most important personal impression will be made via your letter. Your resume acts as a validating document—really just a series of formal footnotes. Remember that your letter is the first (and perhaps the only) indication that your potential employer has of your ability to communicate. If that letter is diffuse, unemphatic, unmemorable, it will have just that effect on its reader. Forget you!

What must the letter include, and how should it be worded?

You must start off by stating clearly the position you're applying for and where you heard (or read) about it:

> This letter is in response to your ad in the Sun-Times for a Manager of Personnel Records.

Remember that the potential employer (your reader) may have used more than one medium in her search, and she may be evaluating the performance of the media for future reference. If you start off by helping that evaluation, you'll be able to ask for fuller concentration during your real personal sales pitch.

Focus

There are two foci in your letter: you and the job. No others must be allowed to detract from these. No discussion of how seldom you apply for jobs from the paper; no explanation of how dissatisfied you are with your current job; no gushing about how you've always wanted to work for XYZ Corporation. You must take what you know about the job (principal description from the ad, whatever solid information you got from the rumor mill), and apply it to your own abilities and ambitions. Period. Say what you can do, what you think the job should do, and quit. Your letter should be no more than one page long.

Mood

Your mood should be independent, aggressive, and self-confident. Use only active verbs in short sentences. Follow these three rules as closely as possible:

1. no words of more than three syllables

2. no sentence of more than twelve words
3. no paragraph of more than four sentences

Your letter must be easy to read. It should contain no professional jargon other than that which is absolutely essential to the subject matter. Remember that the person who does the hiring may not be expert in the field—that may well be why he needs a new employee. Look back at chapter 5 ("Decisions, Decisions"), and make each decision in writing.

Quantity of Information

Remember that the resume is there to provide detailed information about your background and your aspirations. Never make a complete statement about anything in your past in the letter of application; relate everything to the resume:

> As the resume indicates, my position at Universal Playthings involved some management development training in specific subject areas. That training was well received, and seemed to produce some immediate, measurable results.

For the reader to understand fully what you're talking about, he must refer to the resume. What you're aiming for is to get him to read both the letter and the resume fully, but you must lead him back and forth. You must be the master of the message you're sending; that means using a certain amount of methodical planning about the placement of information.

References

If you have excellent references, include one or two in your letter—at the end. Each should be accompanied by a phone number:

> I'm sure that John Alden (215-567-8765) or Priscilla Mullins (215-567-8766) would be happy to support what I've been saying.

The phone number indicates that you aren't timid about using these references, that you're sure about what will be said. The employer will probably not use them (they rarely do, anyway), but he will note the straightforward way in which you offer them.

Salary History

The purpose of including a salary history is to prevent embarrassment. You don't want to be offered a job at less than you're making. Then you'd be in the awkward position of turning down something you originally asked for. The employer doesn't want to waste time with someone who's priced out of his league. The shortest salary history that will satisfy those two goals is the one to use:

> As to salary, I started at Magic Widgets in 1965 at $175/week; my current salary-benefits package is about $23,000/year.

Current Employer Status

It's generally a good idea as well to tell your reader whether she may contact your current employer for references:

> I prefer that my current employer not be contacted unless a job offer is imminent.

or

> You may contact my current supervisor, Tom Brown, but I'd appreciate your keeping this application confidential if you do so.

Put It Together, and What've You Got?

Your best chance. What more can you ask? Mail it and hope.

Exercises

This section has addressed the situation of finding a job, assuming you're looking for one. You may be either employed or in the labor market. There are two other situations that we address in the following exercises.
1. You may be one of the many who look at the *Wall Street Journal* or other job advertisement marts. You may have seen an ad that interested you, but you didn't feel that a response was worth the effort. To practice what we've presented in this chapter, you need actually to do it. You need to respond to several (say three) ads or opportunities you hear about. In doing this, you should keep in mind the following:
    a. Make sure the job and location interests you, so that if the offer were right you would seriously consider it.
    b. In letters and interviews, indicate interest but avoid implying automatic acceptance of the offer to come.

c. It's bad form to accept an offer and then later back out. Word of this gets around and will hurt you later.

d. Don't take the process too seriously if nothing comes of it.

2. Now suppose you're working for an organization that regularly posts job openings (for real) and attempts to fill jobs from within the organization. Over a period of six months you should apply for three or four of these jobs. Again the jobs must interest you and you need to have the proper qualifications. This is excellent practice. Usually you have to complete a form that asks you to indicate how your qualifications fit the job description. This exercise does several things for you. First, you get exposure to people in other parts of the organization. Then, if you don't get that job, you might get another at a later time. Second, you get experience in interviewing and job applications. Third, you can assess the degree to which your skills can be used in other parts of the organization. Fourth, and most important, you just might get the job.

3. We referred to personnel agencies in the book but didn't go into detail. If you don't want to use the routes in exercises 1 and 2, this is a different area in which to test yourself. There are some reasons for trying this out even if you have the other methods available and are happy about your job. You can approach a personnel agency with the view of moving up to a more responsible position or working in a different industry or job category. You wouldn't be expected to have contacts. That's what the agency does for you. They act as a marriage broker between you and client companies. The companies most often pay the fees—usually a flat rate or a fraction of the salary of the person being placed (such as two months pay). Such agencies are valuable to you if they have contacts. But beware: there are also advisory services that do career counseling. These are very different from personnel agencies. The laws require them to state in their ads "not a placement service" or similar words.

INDEX